As a dad and as a husband, I want to do everything I can to protect my family. This book offers great insight to help prevent physical and spiritual attacks from outside influences and is an incredible resource to help those already in the battle. It's a message of hope for all parents.

—MICHAEL W. SMITH, SINGER/SONGWRITER

This is a must-read for  ister, and educator. It brings to ligh ciety has to deal with in one way ne of the predator. Whether it emerges in the form of a person, a drug, or a challenging disorder, the predator still comes to steal the hearts of children away from their families.

The Cherrys' painful struggle and ultimate victory provide practical insight and wisdom to help you avoid the battle...and hope for those who find themselves in the midst of it. I highly recommend it.

—DARLENE ZSCHECH, SINGER/SONGWRITER

A must-read for parents who want a glimpse of our declining culture's intrusion into a Christ-centered family and how God miraculously brought them through it.

—RON LUCE
DIRECTOR, TEEN MANIA MINISTRIES/ACQUIRE THE FIRE

While many families sweep issues under a rug, this family chose to sweep their daughter up in a life-changing tidal wave of mercy and grace instead! Through this book, you'll be challenged and inspired to let God work through you in the lives of your children, no matter what kind of battles they face in life!

—SHANNON ETHRIDGE, M.A.
LIFE COACH AND BESTSELLING AUTHOR,
EVERY WOMAN'S BATTLE SERIES

Unmask the Predators is a must-read for parents who are serious about their role in the lives of their children. This wonderful book is a godsend in our day and age of perversions and abuses of all kinds. Seen through the eyes of an abused and confused teenager as well as through the eyes of a mother (and family) not willing to give up on their child, this book will bring to light vital truths to help any parent wage war against the enemy who desires to break down communication and bring destruction to every family. I strongly urge you to read this timely book.

—DENNIS JERNIGAN
WORSHIP LEADER/ ARTIST/AUTHOR/MINISTER

I will never forget the night Doug Cherry tapped my husband's shoulder during a meeting and said, "We need your help. Please come with me." We followed him to a secluded part of the building where we found Lisa, holding their newborn child, and their oldest daughter, Kalyn. We had never met Kalyn before, but it was obvious something was very wrong.

Lisa fell into my arms sobbing as she tried to explain what had happened. The report was difficult to comprehend. The circumstances were unbelievable and totally foreign to me. Kalyn was involved in a bad relationship, a "computer relationship," which had totally taken control of her life.

Light penetrated darkness that night as a battle began in the spirit to rescue Kalyn from a force she had totally embraced and was unwilling to walk away from. Lisa and Doug were amazing and unrelenting in their fight against the evil that held Kalyn deceived and imprisoned in her mind.

This book is a must-read for parents today who have wrestled with nagging questions of "What happened to my child?" or "Where did my child go?" Though circumstances may differ, the solutions, steps, and tools contained in this book will enable them to gain the victory over their situation as well.

In Mark 9:23, Jesus said, "*If you can believe, all things are possible to him who believes.*" This family believed, even in the toughest of times. They remained faithful to see and employ God's wisdom and today share the testimony of every family member walking in the fruit of this scripture."

—PAM MICKLER
COPASTOR, VICTORY CHRISTIAN CENTER, LAFAYETTE, IN

As pastors, former youth pastors, and parents of a daughter, we found Lisa and Kalyn's book to be both informative and timely. We are grateful that the Cherrys have been so transparent and honest about Kayln's secret and the process they walked through as a family to receive healing and restoration. We highly recommend this book to any parent, youth worker, or pastor. It will open your eyes to the all-too-prevalent problem of sexually abusive relationships and how to detect and deal with it in a Christlike manner.

—HAL & LISA BOEHM
LEAD PASTORS, SUMMIT CHURCH, ELKINS, WV
DIRECTORS OF CATCHFIRE! MINISTRIES

Parenting is not an easy task, but Doug and Lisa Cherry make it look simple. They are loving parents who are committed to raising their children to be close to God. Yet, in these modern times, even the best families face dire attacks from the pits of hell. In this powerful book, Lisa explains how Satan attacked her daughter Kalyn. With heartfelt simplicity and profound insight, this book reveals how a family can emerge victorious from even the worst circumstances. The story of what the Cherry family went through will help you raise your family.

—DANIEL AND JESSICA KING
MISSIONARY EVANGELISTS, KING MINISTRIES INTERNATIONAL

In *Unmask the Predators*, Kalyn and her mom rip the blinders off our eyes, showing us a darkness we do not see and give concrete answers. Sharing their own guilt and confusion, they open their wounded souls until we actually feel their pain and weep with them as they share the dark night of a family's soul that lasted for years; and yet by following "The Plan" God laid out for them, they walked through in glorious victory.

This book should be mandatory reading in every school of ministry everywhere. It should be required reading for every minister, minister's wife, teacher, youth leader, every preteen child, every church membership class, every premarital counseling; and certainly every parenting class should use it as a study guide.

I want all of my children and sixteen grandchildren to read it. I wish with all my heart that I could have read it twenty-five years ago when a sexual predator/youth leader stole the childhood of two of my children…but like Lisa Cherry…I didn't know. But *now* we can know. Read this book and it will change your life and save future generations for the glory of God.

—WANDA WINTERS-GUITIERREZ
AUTHOR, *THE SEARCH FOR PEACE:*
A WOMAN'S GUIDE TO SPIRITUAL WHOLENESS

Think this couldn't happen to you? Think again. I have referred to the crucial teachings in this book repeatedly throughout my own battle for our teenager's soul. This book will give you the confidence to resist the enemy with mountain-moving faith and a steadfast heart.

—LYNNE DAVIS
PARENT OF TWO TEENS, CARBONDALE, IL

Lisa is a very gifted communicator and mentor. Those of us who have had the privilege of being a part of her Frontline Families Homeschool Moms' Group have greatly benefitted from her years of experience in raising godly children, her relational transparency, and her practical, down-to-earth wisdom! This book is a must-read, especially for strong Christian parents who desire to protect innocent daughters from the subtlety of the enemy's schemes and to equip us to live victoriously in these last days.

—JAN CRALL
HOMESCHOOL MOM AND SENIOR PASTOR'S WIFE
CALVARY CAMPUS CHURCH, CARBONDALE, ILLINOIS

One of my favorite authors said, "God is always speaking and doing great things in the Kingdom. Find out what He is doing and join in." God is speaking and doing great things through the ministry of Frontline Families. The book, *Unmask the Predators* is the evidence. Join in.

—DEANNA COHEN
MOTHER OF FIVE/YOUTH WORKER
REALITY YOUTH CENTER, CARBONDALE, IL

UNMASK
THE PREDATORS
THE BATTLE TO PROTECT YOUR CHILD

UNMASK THE PREDATORS

THE BATTLE TO PROTECT YOUR CHILD

Lisa Cherry and
Kalyn Cherry Waller

HONOR NET
PUBLISHERS

SAPULPA, OK

ISBN 978-1-93-802100-8

Printed in the United States of America.

Published by HonorNet Publishers

P.O. Box 910
Sapulpa, OK 74067
Web site: honornet.net

ACKNOWLEDGMENTS

Unmask the Predators never would have progressed past a stack of handwritten notes without the efforts of many caring, loving saints of God who caught hold of the book's vision to bring protection, hope, and healing to a wounded generation.

To Jacqui, Lynne, Tara, Lisa, Lucas, Nathan, and Pam who endured the countless writes and rewrites of two novice writers: we say thanks.

To Chaz, who believed in this book's potential from its inception.

To Karen, who adopted our project as her own and patiently positioned us for success: thanks for the countless hours of extra work.

To Jake, who creatively drew the heart of this message out of us and packaged it to bring glory to our King: thanks for the chance to launch.

To our church family at Victory Dream Center who prayed, stood, and believed with us for a miracle.

To the Frontline Moms' Group, who willingly became guinea pigs for our first Unmask the Predators study group.

To all our precious family—the Renshaws, Grohs, Cherrys, Davises, and Mohrs: thanks for loving us in every season, every time.

To Adam, for your understanding, support, and strength.

To Nathan, Tara, Lilibeth, Ryan, Lucas, Rebekah, Hannah, Micah, Matthew, Ethan, Lydia, and Josiah, and Kyla: you make our home and our lives overflow with laughter and joy. Each one of you makes us proud!

To Doug—Lisa's best friend, confidante, and knight in shining armor and Kalyn's daddy, carrier, and friend: thanks for inspiring us and encouraging us every step of the way.

And most of all, to our Lord and Savior, Deliverer and Friend, Jesus: thanks for healing our hearts to sing again.

Lisa and Kalyn
Psalm 40

FOREWORD

When I read *Unmask the Predators*, I could hardly put this book down. Not only was it shocking to the core to hear about such a beautiful family undergoing such a horrific nightmare, but I really believe this book has a message for every parent in this hour.

This generation coming up has been shaped by so many outside influences beyond family—Internet, media, culture, etc.—and so we parents face challenges that no other generation of parents has ever faced. Lisa so accurately diagnoses the parent/child conflicts and gives insightful, godly, and practical help to overcome. She has done the research for us and very clearly and strategically maps out a rescue plan to take back our kids! Her background of postmodern and liberal thought gives her unique perspective on worldview that we *must* have in order to raise godly children in today's culture, because the world in which they are growing up is on a fast track to postmodern thought.

Whether you are at your wit's end in your parenting and facing your own "dark night of the soul" or you are just going through the normal but sometimes excruciating frustrations of rebellion with your teenagers, I urge you to open the pages of this book and begin to learn how to get your family back to where God is on the throne! Our children and teenagers are the future leaders of the church, this nation, and the world; so it is critical that we as parents do what is necessary and mandated by God for this day and age to see their generation fulfill their destiny.

—KATIE LUCE
COFOUNDER TEEN MANIA MINISTRIES

CONTENTS

Acknowledgments xi

Foreword xiii

Introduction: Why You Need This Book . . . Even When
You Think You Don't! 1

1 A Perfect Family 5

2 Trapped, Torn, Addicted, and Confused 15

3 The Dark Night 31

4 The Tactics of Deception 47

5 The Strategies of Truth 59

6 The Parent's Place of Authority 75

7 Preparing for Battle—Battle Plan Steps 1–5 93

8 Building Your Strategy—Battle Plan Step 6 109

9 Fighting to Win—Battle Plan Steps 7–12 121

10 My Road Home 141

11 Sexual Abuse 101 155

12 Twenty-Six Keys for Protecting Your Child from
Sexual Predators 171

Epilogue: A Word from Dad 191

Tools and Resources 195

Notes 209

WHY YOU NEED THIS BOOK...EVEN WHEN YOU THINK YOU DON'T!

I probably would not have picked up a book like this a few years ago. *We would never be a family at risk for the attack of predators!* my analytical mind would have reasoned. We were far too protective for that. Limited television, careful supervision, weekly Sunday-school training, scrupulously screened Christian friends, lectures on staying clear of strangers: we had all the wise bases covered. Or so we thought. Somehow our naive protections actually made our daughter a more attractive and vulnerable target. And a sexual predator nearly destroyed her life.

When news of sport coach "favors," clergy "counseling sessions," and teacher-student "romances" hit the media waves, we are outraged at the pain of the children. Innocent lives are plunged into pits of perverse trauma they neither deserved nor bargained for. Our collective hearts scream, "Unfair!" and "Sick!" But, unfortunately, we as parents have not gone far enough with our protest. Even though we have jailed a few pedophiles, we have not unmasked the deceiving forces poised to beguile our kids.

In America today an estimated 1 in 4 girls and 1 in 6 boys will be sexually abused by the age of 18.[1] A family's chance of encountering a sexual molester exceeds the risk of most diseases we inoculate our kids to prevent. That is horrifying. But what about other evidences of the devil's deceptive work in

our midst: 11 percent of teenage girls ages 12–18 report homosexual "girlfriend" relationships; [2] media reports that oral sex
is the new good-night kiss of the teen generation;[3] more than
two-thirds of the buster generation (who are raising kids now)
say living together before marriage is morally acceptable.[4]

I hear the parental whispers in the auditorium hallways
across America. "I just discovered my fifteen-year-old's pornography file on his computer," a Christian mama reports. "She's
always loved Jesus. Now she looks and acts like a prostitute," a
brokenhearted dad sobs. "We just don't know what happened!"

I can tell you what happened! The predators have been
given easy access to our kids. And we adults are behaving
like crazily deceived people. The same behaviors we count as
illegal for fourteen-year-old children are culturally normed
and even flaunted on the Internet newsfeeds of nineteen-year-
old movie stars. At the same time, the age of legal consent is
lowering all over the world. No wonder our kids do not know
they are being scammed. As Christian parents we tell our kids
that God has a plan for their lives. Perhaps it is time to tell
them that the devil has a plan for their lives also!

The predators are not just the psychiatrically diagnosed
pedophiles. The middle-school sex-education health teacher,
the friendly cohabitating young couple next door that your
daughter babysits for, and the clean-cut homosexual teller at
your bank who just adopted a baby from Africa are chipping
away at our core values and beliefs while we naively think our
kids are still with us in the Sunday school. Until we unmask
the spiritual forces working behind those "nice people" and
dismantle their spiritual weapons, we will continue to lose our
children. The wave of guilt, remorse, rage, and grief will try to
crush us as we scramble to recover our families.

Our goals here are twofold. First, we will peel back the
deceptions hiding the predators among us. Second, we will

equip you to win the spiritual battle for your kids' futures. By the end of this book, you will have revelation of three key spiritual concepts that will control our children's futures: deception, truth, and parental authority. You will also be equipped with the practical tools you need to keep your children safe from sexual predators in a world gone mad.

Our family's story is not pretty, but we transparently share our painful errors in hopes that others may avoid the path of destruction. So many good parents are like we were: underprepared for their day of attack. So many are giving up in the critical teen years when their kids will either blossom or wilt. Kalyn and I hope to change that. What special insights can an ordinary midwestern pastor's family offer to other families at war? Mostly this: we have been to the foxhole against a whole host of predatory forces and have come back victorious.

Allow the heavenly Father to pull you behind opposing lines and unveil the forces strategizing against your home. Though the enemy is always working his plan, perhaps new preparedness will foil his best efforts even before they are launched. Sexual predators are not new. Their stories fill chapters of our Old Testament history books; their names were called harlot and adulterer in Proverbs; and their wicked spiritual origin was labeled the city of Babylon in the book of Revelation. God calls each generation of parents to *Unmask the Predators*, discover His power and wisdom, and protect His children. So let's get started right now...

The eye of the adulterer waits for the twilight,
Saying, "No eye will see me,"
And **he disguises his face.**

—JOB 24:15 NKJV (EMPHASIS ADDED)

Chapter 1

A PERFECT FAMILY

There is nothing concealed that will not be disclosed.
—MATTHEW 10:26

Beep, *beep, beep,* my alarm screamed as I (Kalyn) hit the off button before it could wake anyone else. Two a.m. Lying motionless on the bed, I strained to hear any sound of movement within the house. All was quiet. Breathing a sigh of relief, I swung my legs out from under the comforter as my warm, sleepy body braced itself for the cold. The moment my feet hit the floor I quickly and quietly slipped on my shoes and sweatshirt and tiptoed into the hallway. Squinting in the darkness, I made a quick scan of the rooms. Reassured that all of my siblings were still asleep, I padded silently toward Mom and Dad's bedroom. Pressing my ear to the door, I listened for movement. Whew, no sound. So far, so good. Feeling my way through the darkened house, I inched my way to the basement, where my older brother slept. Pausing to ensure the depth of his sleep, I slipped silently through the room and out the creaky door.

Seconds later the cool air washed over me as I stepped outside and crept to the front of the house where Dad's black Grand Marquis was parked in the drive. Why was it always parked right outside my parents' bedroom window? I grabbed the door handle of the driver's side and pulled. The loud click of the door seemed to echo in the night. My pounding heart pulsated in my ears as I waited again for signs of movement. When I felt it was safe to proceed, I climbed into the sedan in search of the small electronic device that seemed to control me. Success! My fingers curled around the cold hard case of Dad's cell phone. Protectively, I drew it close and began my retreat from the car, holding my breath once again as I made sure the car door had clicked completely closed. Why do car doors have to slam to turn the light off?

The moonlight lit a clear path as I walked to the detached garage, holding the prized possession in hand. Reaching into my pocket, I pulled out the small slip of paper. Smoothing out the wrinkles, I scanned the various numbers that had been scribbled down over the last few weeks. Calling-card numbers, hotel numbers from different states, and pin numbers. What a mess! With fingers shaking, I carefully selected the digits I needed that night.

Although only a few seconds passed, the wait seemed like an eternity. Would he answer? My heart raced as I heard the familiar voice on the other line—the voice that simultaneously brought me comfort and torment. A wave of both fear and excitement rushed through my body. Surely no one would ever know...

That Saturday

From the time I (Lisa) was a little girl, I had always wanted to be a mother. In fact, I was known in my childhood neighborhood as being the last little girl to give up playing with dolls. Since my own parents had demonstrated the joys of a loving, stable family, I couldn't wait for my turn to be the mommy. I never dreamed back then how many turns I would have!

I met my prince charming, Doug, over a bowl of grapes in the backyard of my church youth leaders' house. He— the dashing athlete with the promising business career plan—won my heart as we strategized a youth-group football event together. We were married a few years later in my home church. Ours was the rare, fairy-tale perfect wedding with the fairy-tale happy ending.

However, I cannot claim we were a couple without problems. As a product of the "new" Christian feminism and spiritual liberalism of my day, those early married years were not founded upon the true Rock that was sure. Baby Nathan, baby Kalyn, and baby Lucas came along before I had allowed the Lord into those confused places of my heart and mind. But once invited in, His Spirit rapidly transformed our home into a radical sanctuary for His glory. Our wonderful marriage became a powerful force in His kingdom as we committed our lives to His service and His Word.

As only God can do, He changed our family plans. We would serve Him in pastoral ministry as we grew a larger-than-average family as well. So we added to our home and our heart Rebekah, Hannah, Micah, Matthew, Ethan, and Lydia. (An ex-feminist liberal with a bunch of babies. Sounds crazy, huh? But remember, I had had plenty of practice with all those dolls!)

We became known in our hometown as the white-fifteen-passenger-van family with lots of kids who loved each other dearly. Close, connected, honest, talented, well-behaved, clean cut, hard working, and fun—that was the community picture. Pastor Doug's family was the envy of every brokenhearted, fatherless child we ministered to—all the more reason that day in October came as such a shock.

With nine children (at that time) ranging in age from eighteen years to six weeks, every day at the Cherry house was busy, but that Saturday in October was particularly intense. In addition to our usual eclectic mix of diaper changing, laundry, and college planning, we had added in a major packing job. Half of the family was scheduled to depart the following morning for our church's annual leadership conference in Tulsa, Oklahoma. The other half of the clan was preparing to depart for a stay with grandmas and granddads. Having previously lived in Tulsa for five years, visiting there was always a welcome haven of sweet friendships and spiritual renewal. Little did we know that one of those last-minute trip preparations was about to uncover the horrible secret that would soon turn our world upside down.

I was distracted that afternoon with my stack of suitcases. When Doug headed out the front door, he called over his shoulder, "I'm leaving for the office, honey. I've got to pay some bills that will come due while we are gone. See you in a few hours."

I'm sure I must have muttered some mindless reply, so when the phone rang a while later, I was only half connected to his voice on the other end. "Lisa, we have a problem," he said. "I just opened our cell-phone bill, and they say we owe eight hundred dollars! Do you know anything about this?"

His dollar figure instantly pulled me out of my distraction. Back in those days, he was the only member of our family who carried a cell phone, so my answer seemed obvious, "No, of course I do not know. I never use that phone. But I am sure if you keep checking, it must be some sort of billing error." And with that reasonable explanation, I turned my mind back to my packing.

> The bill was filled with one- and two-hour phone calls—all in the middle of the night.

But Doug's more careful investigation revealed a most horrifying truth. The bill was filled with one- and two-hour phone calls—all in the middle of the night and made to either one cell phone number or a list of hotels in the Midwest. When he identified the cell number, he realized it was not a billing error. As he called every family member and individually questioned them, each denied any knowledge. And as the hours rolled by and Doug reconsidered all the data, only one plausible explanation remained.

When Doug walked back in the front door, his serious demeanor alarmed me. He pulled me into our bedroom and shut the door. As my mind struggled to believe what he said we must do, I quietly nodded my assent.

He called Kalyn, our fifteen-year-old daughter, into our room. She sat in the big green chair at the end of the bed, where I had been rocking her newborn sister just moments before. Her daddy looked at her with grief-stricken eyes and said, "Kalyn, I believe you have lied to me. You were the one who placed the calls to this forty-six-year-old man from our church."

In that sickening moment, it was if the girl we had known for fifteen years got up and left our room and a girl whom we did not recognize came to sit in her seat. Her facial features instantly changed. With cold, hard, defiant eyes, she looked back at the father she had always loved and snapped, "Yes, I made those calls. I did it!" And then she fell to the floor crying, shouting, and weeping. "Daddy, it wasn't his fault! Daddy, don't bother him. He's going to come and marry me. You just don't understand! Don't call him, Daddy! Don't call him!"

What happened next was even uglier. Shock, accusations, anger, and crying filled the room. The air was so thick, it seemed I could not even catch my breath. A dad-initiated call to the man served as gasoline on the raging fire. He, of course, denied all responsibility and placed further blame on Kalyn.

Our daughter with a forty-six-year-old man! Our minds could not even wrap around the concept. The pain was too intense to bear. In defense, we hurled our words like swords. I, even years later, don't like to remember what we uttered.

"How could you do this to your father and me?"

"*Why*, Kalyn, *why*? You have now destroyed our family's reputation."

"What else are you trying to hide from us? Are you taking drugs too? Maybe we should take you in for a drug test right now!"

"What on earth are we going to tell our family?"

"Kalyn, you surely know this will destroy our church."

All three of us became locked in a middle-of-the-night sea of emotions that none of us was equipped to understand.

"Isn't this just some sort of odd schoolgirl crush?" my mind tried to reason. If so, then why was the emotional response from our daughter so intense, so desperate, so bizarre? Why was she making ridiculous claims that this relationship was now "her whole life" and she couldn't possibly live without this man? How could she claim that this man would be her future husband? Why was she pushing us away, claiming we just wouldn't ever understand? Understand what? It soon became apparent that innocence—both hers and ours—had been shattered and family trust had been completely violated.

The minutes stretched into hours as a thick cloud of darkness enveloped our home. "Perhaps it's really not so bad," my optimism tried to claim. "Maybe we can just pray, go to bed, and then discover with the morning light that the ominous dark cloud has cleared. Perhaps Sunday morning will just progress as normal with order and peace."

That shocking night we didn't understand that the strange relationship between our daughter and this man was really a case of criminal abuse. *A predator had entered our home.*

We didn't understand the effects of this abuse: the deep, intricate soul wounds inflicted on an adolescent and the shame and self-condemnation that were so carefully concealed in Kalyn behind a confident, bubbly, high-achieving teen exterior; the twisted reasoning and sophisticated denial systems that kept a young mind insulated from ugly truths and memories she had no way of handling; the intense emotional energy it required for a normally honest child to participate in a cover-up that had remained undiscovered for almost two years. Kalyn's mind had been carefully programmed by the perpetrator to believe that she was now the "black sheep" of the family. Her soul was locked in a battle with sexual perversity, and her life had become compartmentalized into multiple lifestyles.

Doug and I hadn't had a clue that we ourselves had fallen prey to the parental version of an incredibly powerful, effective, deceptive, and subtle grooming process that had allowed a sexually perverse man near our daughter. Our own overpowering emotional weights of shame, anger, embarrassment, and confusion taunted us with the hideous question: "How can it be possible that we have not seen what has been happening?"

On that horrifying night, our own parental soul wounds blinded our eyes from discernment and compassion. We didn't recognize our whole family was under the influence of what experts called "post-abuse trauma." Little did we know that it would take us over a year to fully uncover all of what had happened to Kalyn and then another five-plus years for the courts to finish dealing with our criminal case. Nor did we recognize the powerful spiritual forces of darkness that had developed fortresses in our own home.

Sunday morning dawned after nearly no sleep. When the alarm rang, I remember asking Doug if perhaps I had just experienced some kind of bad dream. I had jokingly asked that kind of silly question before, but this was different. I was absolutely serious. My shocked and traumatized mind refused to believe that something this horrid could have possibly happened in our home. Model families simply don't have this kind of problem!

We thought of canceling going to church and also our trip to Tulsa but decided not to—we never had been quitters, and life had to go on. Other people were depending on us, and Kalyn, for some reason, still wanted to go. Perhaps the trip to Tulsa might just snap some sense into the confusing situation.

Our peaceful vacation escape did not materialize. Instead, the absurd situation intensified like a snowball rolling downhill, picking up more strength as it went. Who was this child now living in our midst? Her face was hard, drawn, and pale. With the usual twinkle gone, her eyes were sad, cold, and lifeless. Our normally levelheaded, intelligent daughter was now angry, rebellious, defiant, and withdrawn; even after hours of discussion, she remained stubbornly convinced that her parents were crazy to have a problem with this unlawful secret relationship.

> She remained stubbornly convinced that her parents were crazy to have a problem with this unlawful secret relationship.

Desperate for a Miracle

To recall the memories of those next weeks and months is like looking back on the scenes of a bad movie. Moments of horror stand out, like the day I called a family counselor at Focus on the Family Ministries. After listening to the story of what we knew had happened to Kalyn up to that point, the counselor kindly explained that though there did not appear to have been physical sexual contact in this relationship, the psychological damage caused by the Internet and phone exploitation could be very severe. We would need expert help to pull her out of the depression, rebellion, and premature emotional separation from her family that would likely result—and the recovery could take years.

Or like the days when I couldn't get Kalyn to pull her head out from under her bed covers, or drink water, or take food. I helplessly watched her grow thinner and thinner. I tried all the parenting tricks I could think of, but how do you threaten to take a privilege away from someone who claims she wants to die?

Or like the hours of great pain and torture when Kalyn would wander away from the house. We would diligently inventory the house for missing purses, coats, even kitchen knives, all in an attempt to assess whether she planned to be gone a short while, run away, or hurt herself.

Or like the memories of my forced smiles designed to hide the awful realities of our family's problems from my very frightened young children, who were trying to understand what was wrong with their big sister.

Or like the day we found it strangely comforting to finally have a medical expert tell us that adolescent clinical depression following her trauma could be contributing to Kalyn's angry, defiant behavior and irrational thought processes. Put our child on antidepressant medication? For parents who didn't even use Tylenol very quickly, we were strangely eager to try anything that could help save our little girl.

With each passing day, then week, then month, we grew more desperate for answers, for emotional and physical strength, for peace, for hope, for help—for a miracle.

Points to Ponder Chapter 1

- Predators can sneak into our lives unnoticed by us.
- When unmasked, the predator's force is ugly.
- Predator forces can attack our children through sexual molesters or through a host of cultural invaders.

- Once a predator force attacks a child, it can powerfully alter that child's beliefs, emotions, and actions.

- When a child is under attack, a parent as well as the whole family is under attack.

Chapter 2

TRAPPED, TORN, ADDICTED, AND CONFUSED

The enemy pursues me, he crushes me to the ground;
he makes me dwell in darkness like those long dead.
—PSALM 143:3

[Note from Lisa: Kalyn wrote this chapter when she was only eighteen years old. Even though I had lived the nightmare with her, I was shocked when I first read her raw explanation of the pain she endured. We have preserved her original writing to provide a glimpse into her secret teenage world.]

As a member of a pastor's family, I (Kalyn) found security in our tight-knit clan. Our brood was larger than average in love as well as in size, and for as long as I could remember, family was always the priority. From fun nights at home to summer vacations, we enjoyed being together and loved one another dearly. We had been through our share of troubling times and good times, but in the end, our family always stood strong.

Early in my life, I gave my heart to Jesus, surrendering my future to Him. Having been raised in the ways of the Lord, I learned to live my life with purpose every day. As I grew, I encouraged others in their faith and was alarmed when someone I knew fell away from God. Never willing to be moved in my beliefs, I plowed through life with a passion and joy that was evident to all those around me.

I held many roles in both the family life and in our newly growing church. As an active participator in drama, music, and children's ministries, I performed my duties well and left none to question my devotion. My sophomore year in the Cherry home school was coming along just fine. When left to manage the household, I gave it my all, changing diapers and feeding tots like a pro.

I seemed to be maturing rapidly in all areas of my life. Never afraid to take on more responsibility, I functioned in leadership positions surprisingly well for a fifteen-year-old girl. I was a well-respected, mature, godly, dependable girl and appeared to be confidently on my way to an incredible future full of joy and success. No one could have guessed the pain, turmoil, and bondage that filled my soul or seen the ugly intruder eating away my innocence day after day. You see, this dark world that had overtaken me, this horror that overwhelmed my life, had been a secret for almost two years—but the tip of this monster was about to emerge after years of hiding.

From Darkness to Light

That day in October started out as any other Saturday, which at the Cherry house meant schoolwork, chores, and on this particular Saturday, preparing for our upcoming trip to Tulsa. I awoke and began my daily tasks as normal, carefully masking the battle raging in my inner being until 5:00 p.m. when I received a phone call from my dad. My heart began beating rapidly for I had recently grown very fearful of my father, the man I had once adored. After having been Daddy's dear "K-Baby" for so long, I had been pushing him away from my heart. I was terrified that he would find out my secret one day and discover the dishonesty in which I had been living for so long. I was unaware that today would be the day that my darkness, lies, and shame would all be exposed and brought to light.

The next few hours became a blur, for as soon as I realized what was happening, my mind began to panic and shut down to everything around me. My father had just discovered a large cell-phone bill indicating that someone from our household had been calling a forty-six-year-old man from my dad's congregation every night for weeks. He believed it was a mistake—yet this definitely was not a mistake. It was, rather, the beginning of an ugly unveiling of my hidden life. The truth was that this closet affair wasn't new but had been occurring on and off for nearly two years.

Living this secret life had become the norm for me: putting on a good-girl front during the day and sneaking around during the night. Living a double life, however, was not what I desired. I had been tricked, taken, used—my innocence snatched away. Through this man, my heart had been stolen, my mind confused, and my spirit crushed. Still in some way, the sickening attention had felt reassuring.

> Still, in some way, the sickening attention had felt reassuring.

For many months I had been placing phone calls in the middle of the night to this man with whom I thought I had found love and acceptance. In my naivety, I never doubted his intentions; and by the time they were clear, I was already too entangled to walk away. Talking for long hours every night had recently become the norm. Yet I didn't understand why he was no longer speaking of innocent things but was now speaking of my body as an amusement park, seemingly perfect for his sexual gratification.

Entangled and Awestruck

How did I find myself entangled in such a horrible, strange mess? I remember clearly the spring of a couple years earlier when a new family began attending our growing church. I immediately took a strong liking to these people. They were outgoing, talented, and passionate after God; and I was young, tender, and impressionable. This middle-aged couple's twenty-one-year-old son was exemplary in character, traveling in youth ministry circles that I admired. I looked up to him and wanted to imitate his devotion to the things of God—even to the point of having a childlike crush on him.

The wife was kind and caring to all she came into contact with. She was gifted in children's ministry and served at our church with creativity and dedication. She seemed motherly and committed. The man was a very talented musician who served on our church's worship team with my mom (the worship leader), my older brother (our keyboard player), and me (a singer) and was an incredible asset to our primitive band. Many said this man was a musical genius, and his talents were highly sought out. He was also a well-regarded, seasoned employee of a local Christian organization. All in all, these people were friendly and loyal, demonstrating qualities I had already witnessed lacking in so many, even in the short time my family had been in ministry. Needless to say, I was awestruck.

We had gladly welcomed this family not only into our church but into our lives as family friends. We visited in their home for cookouts and gatherings and hosted them in our home for church events and music practices. It was well known that this family had been through some serious relationship problems, but these issues seemed a thing of the past, having been confronted and dealt with before. It appeared that God had indeed redeemed them from past weaknesses and problems. Besides, helping people get healed from their problems was part of our family's and our church's job.

I thought no more about the history of these people but rather, in a strange way, became more and more connected to them. I tried desperately to make a good impression on them. I faithfully helped them set up their church equipment each week, and I was the first to jump to their aid in public or private. I felt they were a part of me, companions who would always be there.

As time passed, changes began to take place in this family, thus affecting me also. The son moved to another state to attend college. Shortly after, the man and his wife experienced difficulties in their marriage and separated. By this time, I was strongly attached to them and felt personally hurt by these changes. The only member of this family who was left in town was the man.

From the beginning he carried an odd air about him, an air that seemed at times intimidating but always inviting. He appeared to keep mostly to himself but was always ready to give a smile or a wink to me. He had long since paid me special attention in soft, subtle ways. I had felt for some time that we had a special friendship. He would often compliment my singing ability, servitude, or appearance, which didn't seem to bother his wife or son, so I just took it as a normal part of being friends with the family. I felt like my hard work to impress this family was paying off! While it may have occurred to me that it was strange to receive such attention from a man thirty-one years my senior, I brushed aside any concern and took it as though it were normal. After all, I reasoned, there wasn't anything overtly inappropriate about it—just a hug here, a whispered "I love you" there, or an occasional comment about my beautiful smile or hair.

It was only after these changes in this family took place that this man began to carry on an increasing amount of time with me. It was also during this period that he began traveling more for his work. One thing led to another, and soon he and I were chatting online multiple nights a week after he introduced me to the instant-message world available on the Internet. Soon he was not just saying hello and goodbye but was asking me when I would be online and when we could chat again.

Eventually he introduced me to the concept of a live webcam—which I requested for Christmas—saying that it would enable us to see each other while we talked. Next came the comments he made while he watched me live on the web— not dirty remarks but subtle changes so as to dull my senses to his real intentions. Comments about church events and his work schedule became comments about my hair and body, how he missed me, how he wanted to see me and hug me. His remarks at times made me feel a bit queasy, but by this time I was hooked.

In January of that year, my dad stumbled upon some online discussions that had taken place between us. He was very alarmed that we had been corresponding, but he knew little to nothing of the context of our discussions or the frequency of them. Assuming there was no real problem, but still wanting to be cautious, my dad ordered me to stop all personal contact with this man immediately. His reaction startled me, and though reluctant, I obeyed. But the hook had already been set, and the strange pull inside me toward this man only grew.

Though the threat from this man appeared gone, in reality it was still crouching at the door, waiting to devour me. During the spring months, interactions between the two of us were very brief and somewhat rare, only taking place when this man was in town attending church. But in July, I called him along with a list of other people about a church event, and the crouching issue became life size. He told me that he had missed talking to me and asked me to call him again. I felt torn, but the decision at hand had in many ways already been made. The pull was strong, and I gave in. I was already emotionally involved and there was no turning back now. Little did I know what was waiting for me just around the corner.

Living a Double Life

Looking back, I remember being utterly consumed with thoughts about this man. My desire to please him, impress him, and be loyal to him dominated my life. I know that this devastating connection must have been constructed on a spiritual level because the tie was so strange and strong it could not have simply occurred in the natural realm.

I now had the difficult task of splitting my life. I had to keep up my performance in all areas of my outer life, yet find ways to secretly talk to this man who told me he needed me. I came up with creative solutions: I would go grocery shopping for Mom and call him from a payphone or ask to make a phone call at someone else's house and go to a back bedroom. My conversations with him were soon becoming more frequent and lasting longer. He continued to ask me to call him and provided additional ways for me to contact him. He began giving me calling-card numbers so that when he was out of town, I could make the long-distance calls discreetly. For weeks this relationship grew and with each passing day, so did the weight of confusion and guilt that I felt.

When I resumed school in August, I became even more stressed trying to manage my schoolwork while carrying on this secret relationship that was consuming more and more of my time. As I felt overtaken by shame, I began overachieving in all outward areas of my life. I was excelling at an unbelievable rate in school and church activities, subconsciously working extra hard on the outside since I felt so very rotten on the inside.

As the weeks passed, the conversations between this man and me became much more personal. Through the summer, I saw this man at church only a handful of times as he was traveling extensively for work purposes. Yet, whether in or out of town, our phone conversations were still occurring multiple times per week; and the few times I did see him, our one-on-one interactions were intensified. These changes included secret hugging, kissing on the cheek and hands, and tender words exchanged.

By September of my fifteenth year, I was completely consumed with this relationship. The man was out of town again and was begging me to keep calling him. I lost all common sense and began stealing my dad's cell phone to make the calls, now escaping to our outdoor garage to carry on our conversations. At first these were daytime calls but soon became frequent in the middle of the night. My life became even more complicated as I struggled to put on a nice front each day and stay awake long hours each night. As I lay on the cold floor of our outdoor garage night after night, I listened to the graphic sexual discussions by this man, unsure of how to respond. I felt sickened, yet my heart was with him, for I had come to love him deeply—or so I thought.

I grew increasingly confused yet controlled by the very thing that deceived me. My perception had become warped and my judgment twisted. I could no longer think rationally or reason with common sense. My thoughts were spent figuring out ways that I could secretly spend more time with my admirer. He warned me to keep quiet about our "love," and I kept my mouth shut. Since

> He warned me to keep quiet about our "love," and I kept my mouth shut.

he told me that people would be mad at me if they found out, I didn't dare speak a word. I also knew that he would be in trouble if anyone discovered what we were doing, and I felt it my duty to protect him. So I planned how we could continue to speak in secret, perhaps meet in secret, and in the future live life together in secret. All of my thoughts, decisions, and actions were based on this growing obsession.

This addiction controlled my very life, but what was I addicted to? Was I just a rebel, seeking to wreak havoc in my parents' lives? Was I a sexual pervert, looking for attention to gratify my desires? Or was I just a girl who had, in the difficult season of the teenage years, stepped off the path of righteousness and reached out for a counterfeit form of acceptance? I had fallen into a pit way over my head, and it was beyond my ability to climb out. Unable to escape the cycle of excitement, guilt, pleasure, and deception that tormented me, I felt trapped—not just by a person, but by the powers of darkness seeking to destroy my life. I was torn. I had seemingly found the acceptance my teenage heart so desired, but with it came the devastating effects of sexual abuse day after day.

I lived in a fantasyland within my own mind. Whenever my thoughts wandered into reality, I felt trapped in a predicament with no way out. I only saw two options—confess to my parents what was going on or stay in the relationship. Both options had devastating ends, and I knew it. Often playing out each scenario in my mind made me feel like I could not live through either, so I denied both, slipping back into my fantasy world as quickly as possible.

I learned to pretend as though I enjoyed the sexual exploration and desires communicated to me by this much older man. Terrified of losing his "love," I went along with all of his perverted ideas, even when they made me feel filthy, violated, and used. I believed his lie that only I could meet these needs in his life lest he be lonely and miserable. He said that he loved me, and I felt appreciated. Swearing my devotion to him and him alone, I obeyed whatever he said for me to do. Every night, he reminded me of all that he would do for me—come after me, marry me, and love me.

This perverted man had found a way into my young life, shattered my values, and convinced me to believe his sick lies. Yet instead of running from him, I ran to him night after night, giving him my fragile heart and all my trust. I was no longer my own, but I was possessed by this horrific monster whose manipulation had overtaken my life.

This was my secret hidden from the world, the source of my secret pleasure and my inner turmoil. I would do anything to keep it from being exposed, yet deep down I longed desperately for someone to detect it and pull me out of this sinking pit. Even though I had been brainwashed into believing this relationship was normal and acceptable, I felt the pain that this deep violation brought with it. But I was confused about the source of the pain. My thoughts were blurred—was I really just hurting myself? After all, I was the "black sheep of the family," he had said. Perhaps my family was the enemy. They would no doubt reject me if they found out about my "love."

As this abusive relationship formed, my heart had been drawn away from God and away from the safety of my parents' protection. I had drifted from what I knew to be true. Consequently, I had felt heightened awareness to the changes and pressures of the world. As I grew older, the temptation to rebel knocked on my door. And in my weakness, I hadn't turned to the acceptance of my parents or to the true love of my heavenly Father but to the cheap counterfeit which sucked the very life from me—spirit, soul, and body.

Was it only a man controlling me? No, the force that held me no man could establish or break in his own strength. I had opened the door for principalities and powers of darkness (see Eph. 6:12), and I would pay dearly.

Payday came sooner than I had expected. Could it be real? Surely I hadn't been found out. It must be a dream! Was there no escaping the disturbing reality? On October 19, it was indeed real; and after hours of lying and fighting the onset of truth, I finally confessed to the forbidden relationship.

The Aftershock of Exposure

That Saturday night in October was the longest of my life. While the investigation of the situation was made, my parents looked on in horror as I became a different person before their very eyes. I cried out in panic and outrage, begging them to leave this relationship undisturbed. My parents watched in dread as I professed my love and devotion to my perpetrator. My undercover life had been exposed and the misery and confusion that followed were indescribable. An intense battle raged on that seemed to be a battle between my parents and me, but in reality, this battle was waged between truth and deception. Holding fast to my abused way of thinking, I refused to move off of my pedestal of lies. Instead, the hours crawled by in confusion, anguish, and misery.

Sleep couldn't bring me comfort that night. Long hours were spent seeking truth and looking for a quick fix. This, however, was a problem that had developed over a long period of time and would take even longer to mend. I groped about in mental darkness and confusion, looking for comfort but finding none. My head heavy, my eyes swollen from tears, I only wanted relief—but it was not soon in coming.

Over the next few days my behavior changed drastically. That day marked the beginning of a downward spiral that continued for many months. I didn't understand what was taking place. I only knew that I was drowning in a sea of suffering and anguish that I had never before deemed possible. I strangely believed that my life had been ruined since my "soul mate" had been taken away. How could I carry on without him?

In truth, I had been abused, defiled, defamed, and damaged beyond my ability to cope. After having been the object of a man's sexual perversion and mania, I was left with an utterly broken heart and a crushed spirit and soul. Yet only over a period of many months of horror, pain, and confusion would I or anyone else even begin to understand the real story of what had happened to me.

The next few weeks I lived in utter torment. I quit eating and shut down my life, hoping that it would simply end. I lived out my misery under stacks of blankets in my room with the door locked, the light off, and the window covered. For this period of time, I proceeded to live in seclusion and alienation from everything and everyone, refusing and unable to face reality. I fell into very deep depression. I slept most of the time, since sleep allowed me to momentarily escape the grief that was shaking my being. But even when I slept, my mind was filled with terrifying nightmares that often caused me to shake with fear. In these nightmares, my mind wandered to many circumstances, some real and some imagined, but all equally horrifying.

Often I awoke from sleeping all day, only to feel more hopeless than before. My iniquity and pain were more than I could bear. The only prayers I prayed during this time were prayers of fury, begging God to take my life. I wept regularly until my eyes had no more tears to cry and my body had no strength left to sob. The sorrow I felt weighed down my body, soul, and spirit, just as if I was carrying a load impossible to bear. This load was very real—a load of guilt, pain, regret, and anger.

I quickly became numb to everything around me—both physically and emotionally. I didn't have the strength to care what happened. I felt I had been hurt beyond the pain any other person could ever inflict and relied heavily on coping mechanisms to continue my existence. Fantasy, anger, denial, and cruelty were a few of the regulars I used to conceal my inner pain and distract myself from the reality of my disgusting life. Occasionally, I wandered away from home for a day, leaving without notifying anyone. I would find a place of solitude, weep until I had no strength left to cry, then lay down on the frosted ground and sleep. I no longer felt the hunger pains in my stomach or the freezing cold on my skin. I only felt the desperation in my soul.

No one else was welcome in this isolated existence that had become my life. Much like a wounded animal, I secluded myself from the outside world, building strong walls and allowing no one entrance to my heart and soul. I found it more difficult, however, to keep intruders out of my physical surroundings. I dwelt in my own bedroom, emerging only when forced to and usually after a battle. Whenever I was literally dragged out of the house to eat, go to church, or see a counselor, it was only after an intense struggle. Even then, I no longer cared what any person thought about me.

I didn't attempt to mask my pain, so I often walked around with an angry expression, sobbed openly, or just lay down in public places like the benches in the hallways of church. When I did emerge from my dark chamber, I usually acted as if no one was present, completely ignoring any remarks, questions, or comments from anyone in my household. I was cruel and ruthless to every member of my family, acting almost inhuman to them. When I did speak, it was only with outbursts of violent screaming and accusation. I was voicing my anger toward my parents, my life, and my God. I held fast to the lies that my perpetrator had sown into my brain, refusing to believe anything rational.

My father and mother did not know where to turn. I pretended to enjoy making their lives miserable, but deep down I despised myself for it. At times I didn't understand why I behaved as I did. Feeling as though a force beyond myself controlled me, I submitted to it, seeing no better option. I was exploding with anger that had to be directed at someone. The target became my parents, the very people laying down their lives in a desperate attempt to save me, their dying little girl.

They tried everything they believed might restore me. Never willing to give up, they prayed, wept, took me on vacations, gave me gifts, and showed me their love every way they knew how. But they were colliding with a wall that seemed to be growing thicker by the day. Taking me to counselors and psychologists only appeared to strengthen the barrier between my parents and me. Many times they considered homes, shelters, and mental hospitals, looking for anything that would bring me back to reality. Despite all of their efforts, I appeared to be growing worse every day.

Throughout this time, I made several feeble suicide attempts, but these only made me feel emptier. I did find some relief in self-mutilation (cutting). Punishing myself felt good. I found that if my physical body was hurting, I could momentarily forget my emotional suffering. I made a regular practice of cutting my arms and legs, making sure that I suffered intense pain. I knew that I was only damaging myself further, but I didn't care.

My secret issue was no longer just my problem at all. I was now hurting my family, as well as everyone around me, but not because I desired to. I felt rejected beyond restoration and wounded beyond repair. Having been brainwashed into believing that I was a destructive person, I acted like one, destroying everything within my reach.

Now severely depressed, confused, and hopeless, I had no desire to go on. I had fallen too far, lost my reason for living, and turned my back on God. Having given up on everything in my life, I surrendered to the torment that knocked at my door.

The girl who had once been full of life, joy, and hope for the future was now lost. After believing that I was invincible, I had now been invaded and destroyed. The same person who used to encourage others to never give up had now herself lost all hope. My life was now a pile of rubbish, useful for nothing. There was only one chance left for me—I needed a miracle.

Points to Ponder Chapter 2

- Even a normally honest, God-fearing child can be deceived by a predator.

- Predators work their deception by a long, slow conditioning process.

- Denial feels safer for a victim than dealing with the true source of pain.

- Hurting people hurt people.

- A teenage world of torment is neither logical nor accessible to an adult.

Chapter 3

THE DARK NIGHT

It's a dark night, a dark hour.

—LUKE 22:53 MSG

I had known, before that dark hour, about mothering valleys. I had weathered enough tough stages, strange habits, stomach flu, morning sickness, and sibling rivalries to be able to trust God to eventually bring us back up to level ground again. Yet I was unprepared for the relentless force of "the worst of times" that suddenly came upon us—the dark night of our parenting crisis with Kalyn.

After we discovered Kalyn's relationship with the predator, my mind became utterly exhausted searching for answers to a problem far too complicated for it to solve. My own failings and inadequacies were so magnified that they looked insurmountable and hopeless, and I was greatly tempted to give up, give in, or give back. It was a season with time urgency, for a child's life was at stake. It was a time I now call "the dark night of a mother's soul." The phrase "the dark night of the soul" is recorded as far back as the 1500s, written about in a book by that title. I can't think of a better way to explain something that I believe to be of life-and-death importance to parents. Many families will encounter this difficult experience. For those parents who aren't able to successfully navigate a dark night, destruction and defeat can result.

"Wait a minute," you might be thinking. "Why should I read about some other family's encounter with near destruction? I do not intend to ever have a dark night in my home, so this is just morbid talk." That is not a strategy I could personally recommend. Part of our spiritual preparation depends upon our willingness to study our enemy's tactics and pre-plan our response to his moves. In 2 Corinthians 2:11, Paul states it this way: "We don't want to unwittingly give Satan an opening for yet more mischief—we're not oblivious to his sly ways!" (MSG). If we can weather the agony of a dark night in our parenting, we will be prepped for victory.

I will begin by breaking down each of the main words in that phrase as we consider its importance to our parenting.

"Dark"

At the very opening act of creation, God talked about darkness. *"God said, 'Let there be light,' and there was light. God saw that the light was good, and he separated the light from the darkness. God called the light 'day,' and the darkness he called 'night'"* (Gen. 1:3–5). Throughout His Word, God identified Himself as the God who is light as in 1 John 1:5 that says, "God is light; in him there is no darkness at all." And Jesus Himself declared, "I am the light of the world" (Jn. 8:12).

Yet just as God is considered light, there is another who is deemed spiritual darkness and described in Scripture as the worker of darkness—Satan, or the devil. Working with him are the fallen angels, the demons. (Eph. 6:12.) Deeds and acts of darkness, which Romans 13:12 and Ephesians 5:11 describe, simply *cannot* come from God.

In contrast, the biblical writer James says about the Father: *"Don't be deceived, my dear brothers. Every good gift and perfect gift is from above, coming down from the Father of the heavenly lights, who does not change like shifting shadows"* (James 1:16–17).

I like the way this passage is explained in *The New John Gill's Exposition on the Entire Bible*: "God…is light itself, and in him is no darkness at all…wherefore he being holy, cannot turn to that which is evil; nor can he, who is the fountain of light, be the cause of darkness…since every good and perfect gift comes from him, evil cannot proceed from him, nor can he tempt any to it." [1] So the instigator of deeds of darkness is the one whom Jesus calls the thief, who comes to steal, kill, and destroy. (Jn. 10:10.) Is it any wonder the predators work their deeds in the cloak of secrecy and often in the veil of nighttime?

We are living in times of an incredible spiritual battle between the forces of light and the forces of darkness. It is a battle between good and evil; righteousness and sin; truth and deception; life and death. All we have to do to see the reality of it is to look around us. Every human being is operating center stage in the midst of this battle. That's why Jesus, when asked how we should pray, closed His prayer with, *"deliver us from evil"* (Matt. 6:13 KJV).

There's protection and safety with God.[2] However, the world as our kids know it is a much tougher, unsafe place than we knew, even one generation ago. As we keep moving closer to the end of this present age and Jesus' prophesied return to the earth,[3] the battle for our lives and the lives of our children is growing more intense. Jesus spoke of this increase in wickedness and conflict in Matthew 24, and it is happening before our eyes daily.

> The world as our kids know it is a much tougher, unsafe place than we knew, even one generation ago.

Consider these facts concerning our young generation:

- About 20 percent of teens experience clinical depression before they reach adulthood.[4]

- Suicide is the third leading cause of death among teens ages 15–24.[5]

- Cutting or self-mutilation behaviors are increasingly common among today's teens.[6]

- Every day, 8,000 teenagers in the United States become infected with STDs (sexually transmitted diseases).[7]

- Fifty-five percent of males and 54 percent of females between the ages of 15 and 19 had engaged in oral sex in a given year.[8]

- Seven hundred fifty thousand women younger than age 20 became pregnant in the United States in 2006.[9]

- Attitudes and actions of professing Christian youth showed only a 4 percent difference from their non-Christian peers.[10]

The battle cry to save this generation of youth has been sounded across the land. Leading youth ministry expert Ron Luce states in his book, *ReCreate:*

> It's no secret that teens are in trouble today. Hardly a week goes by in which we don't see headlines about teens destroying their or others' lives. We see the effects of perverse rock and hip-hop music, but we don't know what to do. We know that Hollywood and MTV have a grip on our kids, but we have no idea how to protect them. Even good God-fearing parents are seeing their children affected by this culture of destruction.[11]

Our family's crisis was just one of many destructive incidents that leave us asking the tough question, "Did God cause this? Our answer is a resounding *no!* It did not come from God. It wasn't by Him, and it wasn't His will for our family—even though now we are able to see good coming out of the pain of this tragedy. God does not work His plan on the earth by causing sin, perversity, and evil deeds. He doesn't cause people to sin to accomplish His will.

Understanding the source of the dark night is critical because when darkness tries to invade a home, many competing voices of explanation can be heard all around that can frighten and torment a person's mind. To avoid all confusion, remember that:

- Our God is a good and holy God.

- The dark night is an encounter with the spiritual forces of darkness at work on the earth today. Ephesians 6:12 states, "*We are not fighting against humans. We are fighting against forces and authorities and against rulers of darkness and powers in the spiritual world*" (CEV).

- Darkness tries to bring fear.

- Darkness tries to overwhelm our senses.

- Darkness tries to hide its true origin so that we will be tempted to believe it doesn't even exist.

- Darkness can be shockingly dark.

"Night"

We all know that night is a period of time that is opposite day. It is the cycle in which natural darkness rules. However, natural darkness can always be overridden by the introduction of artificial light. Think how much impact one candle or flashlight can have in a room of darkness. Why? Because light always triumphs over darkness! Isn't that good news! So the dark night of the mother's soul is a season or a period of time—it does not last forever—in which spiritual darkness tries to rule and dominate. We can rejoice that God's force of light can always overpower and extinguish it.

"Mother's"

How do we define the term *mother*? One meaning of the Hebrew word for *mother* suggests "the bond of the family."[12] Simply stated, the mother is the one who carries and births forth the new life of a child. In a more complete sense, a mother is one commissioned and entrusted by God to nurture and care for the next generation of young. A mother can acquire her charge by means of birth, adoption, or legal guardianship; but however this relationship is initiated, it is honored by God as a sacred trust of the heart.

Mothering is a uniquely feminine activity not to be confused with fathering. It is compassionate and gentle (1 Thess. 2:7), instructive and fervent. It has a loyalty of heart toward a child, which cannot be easily matched by any other human relationship. So as a mother, I have entitled my phrase "the dark night of the mother's soul" because I know it firsthand. Doug also went through his dark night of the soul, which would be called "the dark night of a father's soul." There is a difference. Doug will talk briefly about his dark-night experience at the end of this book because couples involved in the dark night need to understand their differences. Both experiences are uniquely painful.

"Soul"

As the details of creation unfold in the book of Genesis, God reveals that He created us in His image. (Gen. 1:26.) Just as God is a three-part being—Father, Son, and Holy Spirit—He created man and woman as three-part beings: spirit, soul, and body. (1 Jn. 5:7–8 NKJV; 1 Thess. 5:23.) Our spirit is that part of us that comes to life at conception and lives eternally after death. Our body is that part of us that we can see and touch. Our soul is a little harder to define for it is made up of the mind (our "thinker"), the emotions (our "feeler"), and the will (our "chooser").[13] A battle rages between all three of these parts when our soul is in a dark night. The thinker is in battle with the feeler and vice versa, and the chooser is desperately trying to referee and make right choices. Unfortunately, the deeper the battle, the more difficult the choices are.

Our souls are uniquely formed in us by God as He fashions us in the womb. (Jer. 1:5.) The soul will, of course, be further influenced after birth by our life learning and experiences. Because of this, every soul will respond uniquely to life's joys, questions, and challenges.

The bottom line is the *dark night of a mother's soul* can be defined as: "*a season of time when the mind, will, and emotions of a mother are in an incredible battle with darkness because of her role of mothering a child.*"

Diagnosis and Plans

As you can imagine, over the years I've read many books on mothering and on the birthing experience. You might say I've had more than the average amount of interest in the subjects! I always chuckle at some of the information certain books and well-intentioned childbirth instructors give, particularly the ones who attempt to describe a labor contraction by instructing the father to squeeze hard the leg of the mother to mimic the labor intensity. That's the naive image I took into my first labor experience.

I arrived at the hospital that day not really sure whether I was in labor or not. Today, after ten births, I can confidently tell you that if you have to ask someone if you're in active labor, you're probably not. The warm smile and comforting words of an experienced birthing mother who says to a first-time mom, "You'll know when it's real labor," are so very true. Similarly, if you or someone you care about is in a dark night of the soul, I assure you, you'll know!

The dark night of the soul may be thought of as a "second labor in the life of a child." It is not to be wished for or desired, but neither is it to be ignored or feared. It is not an inevitable part of every child's experience (thank God), but it can be experienced as the result of a fallen, difficult world engulfed in tribulation.

No one ever plans on experiencing a dark night of the soul with their child, just as no one ever plans to experience a heart attack. A prudent response to both, however, would be proper preventative care coupled with a preplanned emergency response.

Oh, how I wish I had been better prepared for our attack! How much needless extra emotional pain I bore. How much needless extra pain I inflicted. How differently I would have responded had I known then what I know now! (That is why I am so passionate to help you, fellow parent.)

> How differently I would have responded had I known then what I know now!

The intensity of that dark night of this mother's soul was almost unbearable.

After Kalyn's shocking disclosure, the dark night I entered was like nothing I had ever before experienced. It was an utterly private world in my mind and heart where my emotions and senses became so pained and raw that they could no longer be trusted. If I were to draw a picture of the dark night of my soul, it would be a circle surrounded by six emotions—anger, guilt, embarrassment, mourning, helplessness, and fear. I remember that sometimes I could travel my circle of soul torment in a matter of minutes, or sometimes I would linger in the different stages for days. For many months I lived in a vicious cycle of pain, unable to break out into the daylight. That cycle greatly impacted my ability to parent.

The Vicious Cycle of Pain

Hot passionate anger rose up in me like a wellspring of death. Some of it seemed to be primitive anger like the kind a mother bear exhibits when protecting her cub. Some of the anger seemed much more complicated. I was absolutely livid at the family-friend-become-predator who perpetrated the abuse. But I was also angry at the unfairness of the situation in which I now found myself, having to deal with a crime's aftermath of mental illness. I was angry at the loss of control over my own life that had become complicated and difficult. I was angry at Kalyn for the wrong choices she had made that caused her to be more vulnerable to the attack on her life. I was angry at the forces of darkness for attacking my child. All of those angers seemed understandable, if not justifiable.

But what about the irrational angers that my mind couldn't justify, like the anger I felt toward Doug when he couldn't convince Kalyn of the truth of her situation or control her defiant behavior? Or the anger I felt at others who made helpful suggestions about what we should do to "snap Kalyn out" of the rebellion and depression? Or the anger I felt at Kalyn for being so out of control and miserable? Or the anger that spilled over at my other children just because they were acting like kids? It was a daily battle of willing myself to forgive others, and it was exhausting work that left me raw and worn out.

On days I lost the anger battle, I would easily cycle into one of my many versions of guilt. Guilt for feeling angry. Guilt for acting angry. Guilt for what I thought I hadn't done to protect Kalyn from this attack. Guilt for all the ways I thought I had failed to mother Kalyn over the years. Guilt for all the ways I had failed to mother all my other children over the years. Guilt for not recognizing the danger signs of the predator. Guilt for not giving the other kids the emotional support they needed during this crisis. Guilt for not being a better wife and doing more to relieve Doug's pain. Guilt, guilt, guilt!

Then embarrassment and shame over our family's current status would rear its ugly head. I was so embarrassed to be living our problems in the public light that sometimes I wanted to run and hide. I was embarrassed that we could neither control Kalyn's sudden change of behaviors, nor could we even explain them to very many people around us, as she was not ready for the sexual-abuse issue to be made public. I, the one who normally counseled others, became the one needing a counselor. I was ashamed of my weak performance and failures in other areas as projects and appointments would just slip my mind or seem insurmountable to accomplish.

The anger, guilt, and embarrassment would then remind me of all the losses we had incurred as a family. A deep mourning—not just a sadness—but a sobbing kind of mourning would grip my emotions. Mourning over Kalyn's lost innocence. Mourning over the lost relationship with her. Mourning over dreams and visions we had had for our family life together. Mourning over lost finances and lost business and ministry opportunities.

When we missed Kalyn at the dinner table or when we couldn't pull her out of her room, my heart would grieve for her as if she were lost. When sometimes the children would forget to set a place for her at the table (since for weeks on end she would usually refuse to come), my chest would feel crushed under a weight of grief. When Kalyn ignored the children or refused to ever hold baby Lydia, my eyes would fill with tears.

A mother's highest job is to care for the needs of her family. I wanted so badly to fix this whole mess for everyone that when weeks stretched into months with no answers, relief, or breakthroughs, I was overwhelmed with a sense of helplessness. I was tempted to throw up my hands and quit, but where could a mother of so many go to quit? I knew that wasn't really possible, so my mind began to contemplate at least quitting my work in ministry. Perhaps, I reasoned, I was no longer qualified for that anyway.

Self-doubt attacked my mind and I began to lose confidence in making normal, everyday parenting decisions. If I couldn't prevent or solve Kalyn's problem, how would I help the other kids solve their problems and help them grow up normally? What if this crisis was really a symptom of some potentially serious parenting flaw in me that would be passed on to my other children?

I remember in one particularly difficult moment, when my emotions were out of control, I told Doug that perhaps he had better find someone else to raise our kids since I obviously was failing Kalyn so terribly. Thank God for a husband who could listen to my heart's pain and yet not take my words seriously! But by that point, every area of life started to seem so overwhelming that a grocery-store decision seemed incredibly difficult. My mind was overworked and tired from too much data, too little sleep, and too much reasoning.

Stuck in the Dark Night

Fear, too, seemed ever crouching at my door. Fear that I wouldn't be able to hold up to the mental and emotional pressures. Fear that we would never see our real Kalyn again or that she would run away from us and live a rebellious, dangerous lifestyle. Fear that she would seriously hurt herself or get worse and require hospitalization. I'd often wake up at night with nightmares about all kinds of awful destructions. I would lie in bed unable to go back to sleep until I could sneak up to her room and check on her.

Most of my fears were, unfortunately, justified. It wasn't the "boogey man" kind of fear that is easier to chalk up to an overactive imagination. We had real, alarming things happening all around us. A girl that has been sexually abused often attempts to deal with her inward pain by what's called "acting out" behavior. Kalyn's dress became very provocative and her demeanor flirtatious and rebellious. Coupled with her obvious physical beauty, she was attracting quite a crowd of the wrong kind. It was like she was wearing a sign that read, "Every wounded, hurting, rebellious person welcome here." She was weak and incredibly impressionable and seemed amazingly oblivious to how dangerous many of these people were. We had to become her safety system, which she greatly resented. Every time the phone would ring for her or I saw her talking to others, I would fight off panic that she would be sucked into a world of evil.

Since she was battling suicidal thoughts and hopelessness, she lived on a strange edge of inappropriate risk taking. This was a hard-to-describe, reckless kind of behavior—like getting too close to the edge of a cliff when we were attempting a family vacation in the mountains or being too eager to be the one to climb up on a roof to retrieve a ball and then intentionally walking over to the edge. I often became afraid I might not be strong enough to stop her from being a danger to herself. And what if her example would begin to rub off on the other children's behavior?

I remember coming to the end of many days raw and hurt and weary. I think I can understand why a hurt animal wants to curl up in a corner all by itself. It must be looking for the space for self-preservation—a place to shut out the danger around and nurse its wounds. I found myself looking forward to bedtime as I cultivated my new habit of sleeping curled up on my side of the bed as far over to the edge as possible with the blankets pulled up all around me. I didn't want anyone to touch me or to come too near. Perhaps that's what King David was experiencing when he wrote:

> Be merciful to me, LORD, for I am faint;
>   O LORD, heal me, for my bones are in agony.
> My soul is in anguish.

How long, O LORD, how long?...
I am worn out from groaning;
all night long I flood my bed with weeping
and drench my couch with tears.
    My eyes grow weak with sorrow;
they fail because of all my foes.

                                    —PSALM 6:2–3, 6–7

I wondered how I—as a mother of so many and helping my husband pastor a growing church—would be able to find a private space of my own to have a dark-night-of-the-soul crisis. I often fantasized about running away, but how, or where? Should I run away and take with me the child who was sick? Or, should I run away with everyone who wasn't sick but in danger of getting sick if Mom didn't get back to her senses? Should I just try to grab my husband's hand and run? Or, should I run all by myself and leave the others to fend for themselves? If I did run away, where should I go? To an island? To a mountainside? Or to a new house with normal problems like sibling rivalry and potty training?

In reality, I couldn't even figure out how to imagine myself some relief. No doubt about it, I was stuck here to go through this dark night of the soul. Desperate, I somehow had to find the power to get out of our mess. I knew my God was able and I even knew He was willing; but I would have to fight my way past the deceptions gripping my mind and release His light in the darkness.

Points to Ponder Chapter 3

- Predators love the cloak of secrecy and darkness.

- Our kids' generation is under major spiritual attack from many types of predators.

- God is light and does not ever cause people to work in darkness.

- The "dark night of the soul" experience is a parent's encounter with darkness because of the battle for the child's life.

- A dark night of the soul is as intense as a labor experience for some parents and kids.

- *Light always dispels darkness! Night is always replaced by day!*

Chapter 4

THE TACTICS OF DECEPTION

O full of all deceit and all fraud,...you enemy of all righteousness, will you not cease perverting the straight ways of the Lord?

—ACTS 13:10 NKJV

In the fourth century B.C., a Chinese philosopher named Sun Tzu wrote one of the most studied military tactics manuals of the ages called, *The Art of War*. One of his most often quoted statements is, "All warfare is based on deception."[1] Great warriors like Napoleon learned his philosophy well. Do you suppose that this unsaved Chinese man's work has stood the test of time because he happened upon an observation of truth? However he arrived at his statement, one thing is certain: warfare from Satan is based upon deception.

The enemy doesn't have any new plans up his sleeve. His basic battle strategy for families is quite simple: deceive and attack the weaker members, throw them into a pit of destruction, then lure the stronger ones into the pit with them. Once floundering around in the torturing pit, he convinces his victims that they are helpless and cannot get out. His hope is that they will eventually quit fighting and simply yield to his plans.

Christian families are a challenge to the devil's kingdom by very definition. And perhaps our enemy sees your family as he saw ours—as a threat. So he searched for and found a weak place of vulnerability in our home to launch his attack (which in this case was our child), employed one of his gullible human predators to do his bidding, and captured our daughter as his hostage. And within days of our discovery of his attack, Doug and I were teetering over the same torturous pit of destruction that she was, tempted to cave in to the enemy's pressures and give up.

Give up? Well, I am not proud of that part of my story either. We serve a Jesus who went to the cross for all our problems so that we would never be defeated, yet the temptation to give in nearly overtook me. Why? Because of that powerful force of deception.

To *deceive* is "to mislead by a false appearance or statement; to falsely persuade others or to delude."[2] The alarming thing about deception is that it is deceiving! Think about it. You cannot self-recognize when you are deceived—for you cannot see what you cannot see. Or, in other words, you do not know what you do not know. Tricky, subtle, blinding, confusing, alluring, and entrapping are elements that describe deception's grip. We should have a healthy respect for its power!

Can you see how the sexual predator must be the ultimate tool of the master deceiver? The predator lures his victim into the trap by deception, keeps them silent by deception, hides his illegal activities by deception, and even protects his own conscience by deception. Wow! If we could unmask how that occurs, we could unmask the enemy's other predatory tools as well!

> Can you see how the sexual predator must be the ultimate tool of the master deceiver?

I am convinced we are in error to think the devil is not a strategist. He is a conniver, a liar, and a thug. Just as God is always working His plan, the enemy is always working his plan. Jesus Himself says the devil comes to steal, kill, and destroy. (Jn. 10:10.) Thankfully he is a defeated foe who leaves signs of his activity—and the Holy Spirit will freely reveal those clues to those who ask!

The enemy's tactics can be seen throughout human history because he is not able to create anything new. To understand them is the first step to being protected from his grip of trickery. Let's look at some of his "Top Nine Tactics of Deception" that work against our Christian homes today. Under each deception are some common ways we hear the tactics voiced.

Top Nine Tactics of Deception

Deception Tactic #1: Satan does not exist.

- "Only primitive and uneducated people believe in Satan. Demons having battles in a spiritual realm? That is just fantasy!"

- "Good people go to heaven when they die—but I don't believe in hell for bad people."

- "Demons were just used in the Bible to explain scientific principles the old-timers did not understand."

Deception Tactic #2: Satan does exist...and he is all powerful.

- "The devil made me do it."

- "Satan has always been too much for our family."

- "I never can resist temptation."

Deception Tactic #3: I can handle this on my own.

- "I am strong. I can figure this out."

- "I am well educated."

- "I don't need anybody's help."

Deception Tactic #4: I am helpless.

- "I never do anything right."

- "I will never get out of this mess."

- "There is nothing I can do about it."

Deception Tactic #5: Moral truth is relative to circumstances.

- "Everyone has a right to their own answer."

- "Wait around long enough and the answers always change."

- "Experts disagree on everything."

Deception Tactic #6: I would never be tricked.

- "I can always tell if someone is lying."

- "I can see into situations quite clearly."

- "I am too smart to be conned."

Deception Tactic #7: Life is all about me.

- "I need ..."

- "I feel…"

- "I want…"

Deception Tactic #8: God's Word is not always true for me.

- "I know the Bible is a holy book, but you can't tell what parts are for us today."

- "Sometimes the Bible has the best answer."

- "I am not a good enough Christian for the Bible to come true for me."

Deception Tactic #9: Everyone's doing it.

- "Everyone cannot be wrong."

- "Just look online. It's very clear what everyone's doing."

- "Popular activity is the safest."

Do you ever hear any of those thoughts rolling around in your own mind? Do you hear any of those ideas coming from your children's mouths? The twisted tentacles of this kind of erroneous reasoning can be very subtle to discern in our midst. Take just a moment and read back over that list again slowly. Our ability to detect the counterfeits of the enemy is critical to our children's protection.

Think back to what Kalyn shared in Chapter 2. Are you able to see how the enemy was working against her? She vacillated between believing she was totally helpless and believing she could handle her problem on her own. She did not see any clear answers and did not believe, even in the face of all the evidence, that she had been tricked. Completely self-driven, she avoided the corrections of God's Word and convinced herself that everyone else around her was doing it. She had seven out of nine deceptions working against her!

From that terrible moment in our bedroom when I first learned of her secret relationship, I was able to easily evaluate all the layers of deception operating in Kalyn's mind. However, it was much later in our struggle before I was able to see some of those same tactics applied differently in my own parent mind.

I remember one distinct scene several days into our parenting crisis. We were in Tulsa at the leadership conference trying to hold our family together in front of hundreds of observing eyes. Kalyn was growing more difficult and defiant by the hour as Doug and I were growing more confused and embarrassed. We found ourselves having a "family meeting" in a back room of the same Bible school at which we had previously taught marriage and family classes. (Doesn't the enemy have a sick sense of humor!)

> I looked at this shell of my daughter sitting before me and was convinced that it was not really her speaking to us anymore.

That meeting with Kalyn proved to be our most horrifying one of all. With very cold, calm, deceived eyes, she looked straight at us and announced that our relationship with her was over and that our family was never going to be the same again. She said that we had ruined her life by the way we had raised her. She declared that she was "never coming back," and warned us that we were destined to lose our other children as well due to our parenting flaws.

I looked at this shell of my daughter sitting before me and was convinced that it was not really her speaking to us anymore. The daughter I knew would never say such horrible things. As our storm now raged into a tempest, whatever spiritual strength I was previously operating with seemed to just run right out of my legs. I found myself weeping and wailing in horror. I even remember literally reeling and staggering around the room in my distress (just like Psalm 107:27 describes).

I said things that contributed to the darkness and trauma of that night. I remember turning to Doug and saying, "That's it. We've got to quit the ministry. I've heard of this before. People stepping out boldly into new works of ministry and then the devil attacks them hard and they end up losing their family. I can't do this anymore. I'm not going to lose my family!" I wept and shouted.

There sat Doug weeping and watching in horror as his daughter seemed totally overtaken by darkness and his wife seemed dangerously close to hysteria with a newborn and a toddler crying at her side. In that awful, unforgettable moment, Doug spoke what would prove to be defining words for our battle ahead, "Lisa, we cannot and will not negotiate with the devil. He is a liar and a terrorist. If we try to quit the ministry right now, he will take our church and our family too. I know that if we'll trust God, *He will deliver us all* out of this mess."

Can you see how Kalyn's struggle had become far more than just a teenage girl crisis? Behind every attempt to deceive "just one teenager" or even "just one dad" is a master plan to destroy a whole family, weaken the body of Christ, inject confusion into the people of God, and shipwreck destinies. Why? Because this is not a symbolic war between good and evil; this is a real war waged one home at a time!

Are the enemy's plans working? Is he pulling our children's hearts? See for yourself:

- Between 69 and 94 percent of kids raised in
  Christian homes (depending on which study

you follow) aren't following the Lord after graduating high school.[3]

- Only 4 percent of this current Millennial Generation (born 1984 or later) have been projected to be *Bible-based believers* as adults. That is an alarming decline from the previous three generations' rates of Bible-based believers:

   - ✧ Builders Generation (born 1927–1945): 65 percent

   - ✧ Boomers Generation (born 1946–1964): 35 percent

   - ✧ Busters Generation (born 1965–1983): 16 percent

   - ✧ Bridgers Generation (or Millennials, born 1984 or later): 4 percent[4]

- Only 13 percent of Millennials (those born between 1980 and 2000) polled consider *any type of spirituality* to be important to their lives.[5] (Note: The actual beginning year of the Millennials generation differs slightly from expert to expert, hence the varying dates in the last two points.)

Seems to me the enemy's strategy is working all too well. What a tragedy! Our unseen foe has waged a successful battle to annihilate the next generation's eternal future by injecting tactics of deception into us, while our generation has been asleep on our watch, enjoying our comfortable luxuries and arguing over politically-correct language. We've silently allowed him to reprogram our children's beliefs. We must wake up now! Our enemy is poised to take over our kids.

We shouldn't be surprised at the level of his onslaught against this next generation. From the beginning of human history, he's always been after the godly seed of a generation poised to usher in great revival and the advancement of God's kingdom. Remember when Pharaoh ordered all the baby boys to be killed at the time of the appearing of Moses (Ex. 1:22), and when Herod ordered all baby boys to be killed at the time of the appearing of the infant Jesus (Matt. 2)?

Since the signs of the end of the age are all around us (2 Tim. 3:1–9; Matt. 24), making the season of His second appearing near, the devil is surely more afraid of this next generation than any other. He has turned up his efforts of attack, unleashing every weapon in his arsenal. He starts by preventing as many as possible from ever even being born. (Interestingly, statistics reveal that each year over one million American women choose to abort their babies).[6] Then he works to unleash massive deception, steal the hearts of those born, and thus *destroy their potential* to be dangerous against the kingdom of darkness. The weapons at the devil's disposal are the many predators upon the hearts of our children such as: violence, sexual perversions, pornography, cults, suicide, false religions, immoralities, homosexuality, and of course the sexual abuser. Instead of just standing by and ringing our hands in despair, it is time for us to address him at his points of deception—at his point of first attack.

Think back again on our "backroom meltdown scene" as our family came to remember it. Remember how I followed my daughter right into the path of deception?. On that particular night I displayed evidence of believing at least four of the ten common deceptions discussed above. See if you recognize them as I do:

Tactic #2 Satan is an all-powerful foe.

Tactic #4 I am helpless.

Tactic #5 Moral truth is relative to circumstances.

Tactic #8 God's Word is not always true for me.

I guess we could rejoice that it was only four out of ten. But can you see how many wrong parenting decisions could be made on the foundation of just a "little bit" of those four? And what about tactic #6 (I would never be tricked), which contributed to my inability to detect the predator standing right beside me at church on Sundays? In our battle to protect our children, what percentage of deception mixed with truth is "safe" to our parental leadership? Obviously, none!

I am so grateful that my confused declarations did not prevail on that deeply traumatic night. Did you notice how Doug's response interrupted my deceptive flow? *The injection of truth stopped the force of the enemy!* Hallelujah!

Just as light always dispels darkness, truth always dominates over lies. To protect our children in these difficult days, we must have the tenacity of faith to ask the Lord to reveal any pockets of deception operating in our home. Then we must intentionally step out of all deception and walk into the *power of truth.* In the next chapter, we will do just that as we dig much deeper into the issue called truth.

Points to Ponder Chapter 4

- "All warfare is based on deception."

- *Deception* by very definition is extremely difficult to detect without help.

- Kids and parents can both fall into the common deceptions of our culture.

- Satan is working overtime to annihilate this generation via deception as evidenced by declining numbers of Bible-believing Christians in our kids' generation.

- Making decisions based on even a small amount of deception is extremely dangerous.

- We must have the courage to allow the Lord to reveal to us our deceptive thoughts.

Chapter 5

THE STRATEGIES OF TRUTH

Everyone who hears these words of mine and puts them into practice is like a wise man who built his house on the rock.

—Matthew 7:24

The two-hour drive home from the St. Louis Airport felt like an eternity to me (Lisa). My heart was crushed and hemorrhaging, yet somehow I was able to smile and carry on light-hearted conversation with our traveling companions while replaying in my mind the tapes of the Bible-school-backroom-meltdown scene. With Kalyn safely asleep in the back of the van, I counted the minutes until I could deposit the whole family back into our six-bedroom split-level. All I could think about was having privacy in our seven-acre home, with its surrounding fields and woods nearby.

Cherry family homecomings are never quiet, and when the van pulled in the driveway, everyone went running in their own direction—some to check on pets, others to unpack new treasures from Grandma and Granddad's house. I grabbed the baby and attempted to hide myself for a few minutes in the master bedroom. My escape was short-lived as my expertise at unpacking was required. After forty-five minutes of controlled mayhem, one of the younger children asked, "Where's Kalyn? We can't find her anyplace."

"I'm sure she's here somewhere," I said with a forced smile. My heart sped up as I hurriedly searched the whole house and yard, then headed outside to find Doug. My words, "Doug, she is gone," surely caused his mind to flood with the same thoughts as mine. We had both witnessed Kalyn's horrible speech to us in Tulsa just forty-eight hours prior, and now she was gone.

Could she have called the man, arranged a meeting, and left with him? Could she have walked down the road to hitchhike or found a way to the bus or train station? Is she systematically working on an escape plan or just randomly expressing her desperate emotions? My first wave of questions was troubling, but my second wave was horrifying. Is Doug's hunting shotgun still in its case? Does she know how to load it? Are there any knives missing from the kitchen? Do we own any dangerous prescription drugs?

Doug drew the same conclusions, for when our son Nathan arrived on the scene moments later, I heard Doug quietly ask him to go get both of their hunting guns and hide them deep within the attic rafters. Nathan, wide-eyed, quietly hurried to obey.

I thought my legs were going to crumple as I fell into Doug's arms, crying. A quiet strength came over him as he gently said, "I was praying about this situation the whole way home on the plane. I believe the Lord spoke to my heart three things. First, He promised me that He is going to bring her out of this. But, secondly," he quickly added, "He also warned me that things were going to get a lot worse before they get better. I just didn't realize how quickly the word He spoke to me would come to pass. We've got to do the third thing He said to do—trust Him and believe His Word as absolute truth."

There it was again...an anchor of truth in the midst of the storm.

For several hours, Doug and Nathan alternated drives down the road with hikes in the woods, while I stayed at home by the phone. We were about to call someone somewhere about Kalyn when Nathan spotted something red wandering slowly across a distant field. As we sat in the living room watching, the red sweatshirt quietly drew closer to the house and slipped into our basement back door. Doug was the first to greet her, but all she could do was walk through the door and fall into a crumpled heap on the floor, quietly weeping. Gone were the angry, defiant teenager and any words of explanation. Now we simply rushed to put blankets around our cold, broken little girl.

A Passion for Truth

The issue of truth was paramount to our family at that perilous moment. We were faced with the option of moving deeper with Kalyn into our own parental version of deception (which would, of course, thrill the enemy of our home), or we could discover the strategies of truth that would release God's miracle-working power into our desperate situation. Thank God, His grace enabled us to choose the latter!

The question pertinent to all of us is, how do we reject the tactics of deception striving to take hold in our homes and rebuild our lives on the truth—especially since the whole concept of truth has been muddied by modern thought? For truth to dominate every thought, every belief, and every action, truth must become our passion.

> How do we reject the tactics of deception striving to take hold in our homes and rebuild our lives on the truth?

Postmodernism, a descriptive word used to describe our age, is rarely understood by the common person. Perhaps you are like me and the discussion of such abstract philosophical ideas seems academic and mostly irrelevant. However, since we have witnessed such a staggering shift in the belief systems of our age, perhaps we need to pause long enough to gain understanding. David Kinnaman of Barna research says his investigation "paints a compelling picture that moral values are shifting very quickly and significantly within the Christian community as well as outside of it."[1]

Postmodern philosophy has created a whole generation of teens who believe that "truth is not true for them until they choose to believe it."[2] Josh McDowell, the renowned apologist and expert in the youth culture, states:

> So, while postmodernism is tough to pin down, it is possible to summarize its most common beliefs:
>
> Truth does not exist in any objective sense.
>
> Instead of "discovering" truth in a "metanarrative"— which is a story (such as the Bible) or ideology (such as Marxism) that presents a unified way of looking at philosophy, religion, art, and science—postmodernism rejects any overarching explanation of what constitutes truth and reality.
>
> Truth—whether in science, education, or religion—is created by a specific culture or community and is "true" only in and for that culture.
>
> Individual persons are the product of their cultures. That is, we are not essentially unique individuals created in the image of God; our identities are defined by our culture (African-American, European, Eastern, Western, urban, rural, etc.).
>
> All thinking is a "social construct." In other words, what you and I regard as "truths" are simply arbitrary "beliefs we have been conditioned to accept by our society, just as others have been conditioned to accept a completely different set of beliefs."
>
> Any system or statement that claims to be objectively

true or unfavorably judges the values, beliefs, lifestyle, and truth claims of another culture is a power play, an effort by one culture to dominate other cultures."[3]

This understanding of truth wreaks havoc over our homes. But the debate over the concept of truth is nothing new. While our postmodern philosophies may be pressuring us to give up on the concept of absolute truth, Adam and Eve knew that same deceptive pressure in the garden of Eden when the serpent said to them, *"Did God really say, 'You must not eat from any tree in the garden'?"* (Gen. 3:1). Pilate at Jesus' trial knew that same struggle when he asked the profound question, *"What is truth?"* (Jn. 18:38. See also Jn. 19:1–16.)

Can you see what we are up against in our homes? Only the power of the Word of God will penetrate the deception that undermines our cultural receptivity to the concept of truth!

Do you have a passion for truth? Is it burning in your heart? Are you willing, if needed, to be the only family on the block to regain your foundation in the kingdom of light and confirm a belief in truth? Doing so is our only hope against the onslaught of all the predators.

To drop an anchor in our homes, our next step is to go back and look at those Top Nine Tactics of Deception we identified in chapter four and boldly replace them with the *Word of truth.*

The Nine Strategies of Truth

Deception Tactic #1: Satan does not exist.

TRUTH STRATEGY #1: *"Be self-controlled and alert. Your enemy the devil prowls around like a roaring lion looking for someone to devour"* (1 Pet. 5:8).

For years I fell for the deception that the devil does not exist, as do many non-Christians and Christians alike. Studies by the Barna Research Group in 2009 indicate that only about 35 percent of polled *adult Christians* believed that Satan is a real entity.[4] That represents a dramatic shift in the body of Christ.

How's that for an effective strategy? Kind of reminds me of the silly occasions when my kids have plugged their ears to pretend like they did not hear my voice calling. The devil is real. He has a voice. And he is calling.

Deception Tactic #2: Satan does exist…and he is all powerful.

TRUTH STRATEGY#2: *"The reason the Son of God appeared was to destroy the devil's work"* (1 Jn. 3:8).

Intimidation can paralyze the army of God today as it did in Israel during the time of Goliath. Satan does have power, but he is not omnipotent (all powerful). He was defeated at the cross and we, as believers, overcome him by the blood of the Lamb and the word of our testimony. (Rev. 12:11.) For Christian parents to cower in fear of predators is not proper. We must face them the same way Jesus faced the forces of darkness attacking Him in the wilderness (Lk. 4:1–13), through the powerful sword of truth, the Word of God.

Deception Tactic #3: I can handle this on my own.

TRUTH STATEGY #3: *"Apart from me you can do nothing"* (Jn. 15:5).

The phrase "God helps those who help themselves" is not found in the Bible. Yet many of us act like it is with our rugged individualistic approach to our Christian lives. Even with a measure of the fear of God, we can easily fall into a foolishly independent spirit that causes us to either intentionally or accidentally violate the Word and will of our Father.

My early parenting years were filled with this deception. I was driven to be a "good parent," but I was consulting the modern child-raising experts who were *not* consulting the Lord! My own fleshly mind can always invent a new idea. The experts on the Internet can easily invent a dozen. I believe some of the worldly decisions we made in Kalyn's early years could have contributed to her vulnerability of attack in her adolescence. All foundations from childhood are tested in the teen years.

What freedom came into my life when I intentionally transferred the decision-making weight from my shoulders to the Holy Spirit, my wise counselor! For we can be confident when the Spirit of truth comes, He guides us into all truth. (Jn. 16:13.)

Deception Tactic #4: I am helpless.

TRUTH STRATEGY #4: "*My help comes from the* LORD, *the Maker of heaven and earth*" (Ps. 121:2).

The deception that we are helpless could actually be true…if we have not surrendered our lives to the Lord Jesus Christ! We can read all the latest and greatest techniques to protect our homes; but dads, moms, teens, and kids are hopeless and helpless to escape the grip of darkness without God.

Nothing will drive a parent to their knees faster than a crisis with their own precious child. And nothing will reveal the status of our own parental spiritual condition faster than a crisis with our own child. Have you ever noticed how many praying folks you discover in a children's hospital? Anyone can throw a prayer up to the Lord, but only the prayers of the righteous man are powerful and effective. (James 5:16.) Our covenant—or lack of covenant—with God makes all the difference to our parenting.

Two Important Greek Words

God never intended His people to be helpless on the earth. An understanding of two Greek words used in the New Testament, *exousia* and *dunamis*, were critical to Doug and me that day we stood in our driveway talking about hiding Doug's hunting guns, and they are just as important today when we make decisions for our younger children. I feel it is vital that we digress a moment to understand their significance.

Exousia refers to force, superhuman mastery, and delegated influence, which reflect authority.[5] In the New Testament, *exousia* is translated "power" 69 times, "authority" 29 times, and "right" 2 times.[6] No doubt the people of Jesus' time clearly understood this robust term. So when Jesus was described as having *exousia*, naturally He upset the religious leaders. His teaching had *authority*. His miracles demonstrated His *power*. And He was clearly establishing His *rightful place* of Lordship.

On the other hand, Jesus' mission was not just one of demonstration—it was also one of restoration. He gave His authority back to His children—which includes us! At one point He "*summoned His twelve disciples and gave them authority [exousia] over unclean spirits, to cast them out, and to heal every kind of disease and every kind of sickness*" (Matt. 10:1 NASB). In speaking to the seventy-two followers He sent out in Luke 10:19, Jesus said, "*Behold, I have given you authority [exousia] to tread on serpents and scorpions, and over all the power of the enemy, and nothing will injure you*" (NASB). And at His closing exhortation to His disciples in Matthew 28:18 He said, "*All authority [exousia] in heaven and on earth has been given to me. Therefore go and make disciples of all nations.*"

Clearly Jesus had the *exousia,* and He transferred the *exousia* to His true followers. God said of Jesus through John, "*To all who received [Jesus], to those who believed in his name,* _____ power, authority—exousia] to become chil-_____ 12). This verse reveals who has the privilege _____ spiritual forces of darkness: the *children of* _____ s we must have repented of our sins, _____ s our personal Lord and Savior, and been _____ dom by the new birth. (Jn. 3:3; Acts 2:21.)

> Facing the predators of our generation without the *exousia* from the Lord would be stupid and dangerous!

Facing the predators of our generation without the *exousia* from the Lord would be stupid and dangerous! If you are not confident of your personal relationship with the Lord, today can be your day of salvation. Humble yourself before Him. Repent of your sins. Ask Jesus to become the Lord of your life and believe in His resurrection power. For more help and information, please refer to our website—Frontlinefamilies. org—and click on the "Jesus" button.

Once we know we are in right standing with God because of our new-birth covenant, we, as parents, can shake off our fearful wimpy leadership and take our position in prayer against the predators. We are no longer powerless! This brings up the second Greek word that greatly aided Doug and me in our battle: *dunamis*. It is one of the words translated "power" in the New Testament. It is that explosive, supernatural, victorious, dynamite-like power that raised Jesus from the dead as referred to in Ephesians 1:18–19. In fact, Paul prayed that we would *know* that kind of power, that is, that we would have a practical, working knowledge of it in our everyday lives. Parents, to rescue this troubled generation, we will need a full load of *exousia* (His authority) and *dunamis* (His power) to proclaim, *"Satan, I command everything being done in darkness in my home to come into the light, and I demand you and all your forces to leave my home in Jesus' name!"*

Deception Tactic #5: Moral truth is relative to circumstances.

TRUTH STRATEGY #5: *"Jesus answered, 'I am the way and the truth and the life. No one comes to the Father except through me"* (Jn. 14:6, emphasis added).

Deception Tactic #5 may be the granddaddy of them all. We could say that all of life hinges upon its issues. Is there one truth or multiple truths? Jesus' words should be our simple anchor. He is not one of many truths—He *is* truth.

Our world is spinning out of control because the devil has succeeded incredibly in the last generation to sell this deception. Consider these facts:

- Seventy percent of youth say there is no absolute moral truth.

- Eighty-one percent of our kids claim, "All truth is relative to the individual and his/her circumstances."[7]

And if we are looking for the adults to stabilize this sinking ship, better think again:

- Only 9 percent of all American adults have a biblical worldview.

- Only 34 percent of American adults believe that *moral truth is absolute* and unaffected by the circumstances.

Or if we are looking to the *Christian* adults to solve the issue, we need to assess ourselves again as:

- Only 46 percent of born-again believers, according to Barna's research, believe in absolute moral truth."[8]

No absolute truth? That is absolutely incompatible with biblical teaching! God, as our loving heavenly Father, would never leave His children in such confusion. He gave us His Word to show us the truth that we may live orderly and free lives. It is the enemy of our souls who has attacked the integrity of the Bible so that he can ultimately steal our souls, pull us into immorality, and destroy our children.

Some said to us when they heard of Kalyn's story, "Doug and Lisa, don't get your hopes up. There are no clear answers for these kinds of problems. She will probably never fully recover." But we refused to believe the deception that we could not find God's solutions to our multiple, complex problems. We knew it would not be easy. We knew it would take time and extreme wisdom from the Lord. But we believed in the power of *truth* to set her free—and now our daughter is healed! We must not give into this deception of "no absolute truth," lest we miss our God's voice.

Deception Tactic #6: I would never be tricked.

TRUTH STRATEGY #6: "*Pride goes before destruction, a haughty spirit before a fall*" (Prov. 16:18).

"*Therefore let him who thinks he stands take heed lest he fall*" (1 Cor. 10:12 NKJV).

This surely was one of the most serious deceptions we had prior to the predator's attack. The truth is, I am *not* always able to see or discern the whole truth of a situation with my natural eyes or my human mind. Even my young children can sometimes trick me with a "magic" card trick. Certainly, professional con artists could trick me with their skilled deceptions. But even more, I realize I am only cognizant of but one dimension of reality, the physical realm. My natural eyes are unable to see into the spiritual realm of the second heaven.

I was never more keenly aware of this fact than during our struggle for Kalyn. We were fighting against powers much stronger than the emotions of a confused fifteen-year-old girl. The truth of Ephesians 6:12 became quite apparent: "*Our struggle is not against flesh and blood, but against the rulers, against the authorities, against the powers of this dark world and against the spiritual forces of evil in the heavenly realms.*"

Kalyn had been "soul tied" to a man steeped in the dark world of pornography and perversion. The battle for her life *was* a battle in the heavenlies. My busy bluster of motherly activity highlighted with my angry yells of correction did no good. But once we began resisting him in prayer with the power of the Word of God, we began to see our situation change.

Now I regularly ask myself, "What distractions of everyday life and what noise from the technology machine are blinding you from the activities in the spirit realm, Lisa?" That question alone drives me to my heavenly Father in utter humility. For how can I see what I cannot see if not by receiving wisdom through His eyes?

Deception Tactic #7: Life is all about me.

TRUTH STRATEGY #7: *"Then he said to them all: 'If anyone would come after me, he must deny himself and take up his cross daily and follow me. For whoever wants to save his life will lose it, but whoever loses his life for me will save it'"* (Lk. 9:23–24).

As we have grown fat on selfish comforts, we in our modern age have allowed our stuff to fool us into the idolatry of self-worship. As Ron Luce stated,

> The culture machine is not just media, it is stuff—stuff to see, stuff to watch, stuff to go to, stuff to wear, stuff to give, stuff to drink, stuff that makes you pretty, stuff that makes you cool, stuff that makes you popular, stuff that makes you sexy, stuff that is fun to do, stuff that is adventurous, stuff that will live your life for you so you don't have to go anywhere or do anything. Our lives are filled with *stuff.*[9]

And I came to realize that all that stuff is about me, my pleasure, and my feelings! Ugh!

Deception Tactic #8: God's Word is not always true for me.

TRUTH STRATEGY #8: *"Then Peter opened his mouth, and said, Of a truth I perceive that God is no respecter of persons"* (Acts 10:34 KJV).

The nature of truth is its universality. It could not be truth if it only stood on some days or for some people. It is true that God's promises are conditional—but that condition is related to our covenant relationship with Him. Being born into the kingdom of God has extreme benefits! Once we become His child, He allows *all* of us to partake freely of His Word, which is filled with promises.

We can play by His kingdom rules and reap the rewards of His kingdom blessings or not play by the rules and miss His blessing. The choice is ours. But it is not truth to accuse God of favoritism. He is completely perfect and just. (Deut. 32:4.)

Deception Tactic #9: Everyone's doing it.

TRUTH STRATEGY #9: *"Enter through the narrow gate. For wide is the gate and broad is the road that leads to destruction, and many enter through it. But small is the gate and narrow the road that leads to life, and only a few find it"* (Matt. 7:13).

Obviously, this scripture warns us about following the crowd. Jesus is clearly showing us that many will be tricked out of their own salvation because of following their own way. Surely we have seen this truth demonstrated in history as whole nations were deceived into holocaust activity.

Perhaps you have used this reasoning when discipling your own children: "So, son, if everybody was robbing a bank, would you do it too?" We know that is goofy logic, yet we still have a hard time resisting the pull of popular opinion.

We must rise up in these latter days with a different spirit about us. What if *none* went with you? Would you still follow? Are you personally prepared to stand in the minority with the

Lord? How about your children? Are you aiming your whole family toward being part of the Lord's end-time remnant?

Remnant talk changes everything about our priorities and decisions. If it is true that Jesus will come back for a church who will not be the popular majority, perhaps we need to check our lives to see if we *are* flowing in the mainstream and *not* in the remnant.

The Truth Conclusion

Doug and I knew our only hope in saving Kalyn was to completely acknowledge every false belief that polluted our hearts as parents and allow the Lord to search us regularly for the arrows the enemy would try to re-inject into our minds. We know personally that families can be delivered from even the deepest darkness and pain. But even more, we can attest to the imperative work of continually allowing the Lord to search us for any trace of these nine deceptions!

Right now we have five teens and preteens in our home with two more still coming up behind. We will need more of His grace-filled power in our parenting than ever before if we are to escape the deadly arrows from the kingdom of darkness. As we humbly seek God's truth strategies as parents, we are able to take a rightful place of leadership in our home and dismantle every false-faced predator that comes near our children.

Points to Ponder Chapter 5

- Through postmodernism, the enemy has convinced most in our culture to abandon the concept of absolute truth.

- Only the truth strategies of God's Word will dispel the deception tactics of our day that open the door to predators.

- We must cultivate a passion for truth.

- Satan, the master deceiver, has convinced 65 percent of polled adult Christians that he is not real.

- As parents, we have the *exousia* and the *dunamis* to defeat the enemy in our homes if we are true believers.

- Parental pride can lead to a fall.

- We must aim our homes toward being part of God's remnant.

Chapter 6

THE PARENT'S PLACE OF AUTHORITY

[Jesus said,] "I have given you authority to trample on snakes and scorpions and to overcome all the power of the enemy."

—LUKE 10:19

As I awoke one hot, muggy southern Illinois day in July, some nine months into our battle, I proceeded through what had become my morning routine—one not enjoyable but designed to rescue my day from certain disaster. It seemed that no matter how I distracted myself as I woke up, the thoughts of the previous days' stresses and traumas would hit my mind like a runaway freight train. Whatever the cause of my pessimistic anxiety—nighttime dreams that were so miserably disturbing that my brain awoke already fatigued or emotions that were worn and raw—I knew my only ray of hope was to grab my Bible, begin praying, and wrestle my own thoughts into God's order of peace. My kids needed a mama who could face the day with confidence and strength.

As I began my prayer time that day, I knew I had so much to be thankful to God for. Kalyn really was quite a bit better. She had been on antidepressant medication for six months and was no longer clinging to her bed. Her thought processes were much more reasonable. In fact she had, only a couple weeks before, broken completely free of her confusing denial state about the abuse while on a lunch outing with Doug.

On a regular basis for months, we had asked her if she was ready to talk about what had happened with the man. On this particular day, however, she suddenly said, "Yes, I'm ready to talk." Then right there in the car, amidst tears and sobs, the true story finally poured out of her mouth. That was also the day when she said she knew that what this man did was wrong, dangerous, and illegal. She wanted to tell that same story to the police. I was shocked when Doug called me on his cell phone to say they were on their way to the sheriff's department.

As I hung up my phone, I wondered why she suddenly chose that day to share the details of her story. Did she really want help dealing with her troubled world of reality, or was it for a less noble reason? Perhaps she was simply tired of living in a sixteen-year-old limbo state without her driver's license. Her driver's education had been completed for months, but she knew we would not be giving her permission for a license until we could sense she was ready to receive help for her months of trauma and erratic behavior.

Doug and I had struggled over that decision. We hated to disappoint her on her sixteenth birthday or to become the "bad guys" again in her mind and withhold the car. After all, she had been through so much trauma and disappointment. But we couldn't send her out into the world driving a car unsupervised when she was still living in denial. How could we trust that her emotional state would allow her to make mature choices? There was just no way we could hand her those car keys and take those risks. We had to believe that one day she would thank us for our firm, clear stand.

This day, I was thanking God that we had received phase one of the reward for our tough disciplinary stand—her vow of silence was now broken!

Filing a Police Report

The visit to the police station went well. The officer was kind as he gently questioned and probed her story. He did a great job of explaining to her that she had been a victim of a long "grooming process,"—a tricky, subtle, psychological manipulation that had caused her to freely participate with the perpetrator's instructions, while hating it and keeping her vow of silence at the same time. The officer commended her for coming forward to the authorities to tell the truth.

Doug was able to reveal to the police the Internet dialogues Nathan had accidentally found stored on our home computer several months prior. The dialogues contained instructions from the man to Kalyn to "keep our secret," dating way back to when she was fourteen years old. It really seemed to help Kalyn to have someone other than her parents diagnose that she had been a victim of a crime.

Doug and I had talked with the deputies months prior, and they had advised us that there was no hurry to file our police report. In fact, they recommended that we wait until Kalyn was able emotionally to come out of her silence and make the statement voluntarily. Doug had spent many hours praying about whether filing a police report was really necessary for us to do. Would we just needlessly increase our family's pain if we reported the abuse? Shouldn't we just practice "kindness" and all try to "forgive and forget" what had happened? But what about our responsibility to other families and churches who could be affected by this man's unethical behavior?

> As law-abiding citizens, reporting illegal activity positioned our family on the side of truth and justice.

As Doug listened for the Lord's direction in this matter, he became convinced it was necessary for us to make that report to our authorities. As law-abiding citizens, reporting illegal activity positioned our family on the side of truth and justice. And truth would, as we were standing on it and believing, set all of us free—including Kalyn and the perpetrator. What the authorities did with this truth would then be up to them. What we did as a family to release this man through forgiveness would be up to us.

When she arrived home from the police station, she looked like a different child. Though her behavior was still not that of our normal Kalyn, she looked as if some invisible thousand-pound weight had been lifted off of her shoulders. And for the first time in months, she expressed some angry feelings toward the correct target—the abuser—instead of toward herself or us. We thanked God for this breakthrough, yet we knew we had much more ground to take back. It was still too painful for her to tell the officer about the exact details of some of the phone dialogues. More recovery time was needed.

Turning Point in the Battle

As I finished my prayer time that day in July, I was somewhat relieved. My whole family was at least operating in the same world of reality! But while Kalyn was finally able to label the abuse as abuse, she was still very confused as to how the abuse happened. To her, our "oppressive parenting" had driven her to need to be rescued by this man who had become her confidant and advisor. While the same household rules had been normal and understandable to her in the past, now under the influence of full-blown teen rebellion, they seemed tight, unfair, and ridiculous to her. So daily she was suspicious and hostile toward any of them, such as chores, bedtimes, and rules of etiquette.

Everyday life was still very much a struggle. I found myself trying really hard to give as few parental directions and commands to her as possible because I hated the bristling, edgy, surly responses she made to even my simplest requests, things like picking up her coat or cleaning her dishes. Even my motherly presence seemed to evoke hostility. It was a miserable way to live. So on that day in July, my nerves were in the new normal state: raw and preset for battle. I worked hard to cover it all with a smile, but inwardly my spiritual weapons were always in my hands, and my mind was always alert for trouble.

Kalyn had been pushing the line with me all day, challenging my directions and comments. We had entertained a group of her teenage friends as they played basketball and swam in the pool throughout the afternoon. Finally, evening was approaching and I was about ready to be done entertaining. Little did I know the greatest demand on my parenting for the day was just beginning.

Later that afternoon, after the guests had left, a car pulled in the driveway that I did not recognize. I had, however, seen a couple of the car's passengers before. A sick feeling immediately hit the pit of my stomach. My mind began racing as my pulse began rising. Immediate warning alarms were screaming in my head. One look yielded a quick diagnosis. These new kids were clearly trouble, and it appeared they wanted to escort Kalyn into trouble with them.

I watched out the window as Kalyn began chatting animatedly with the driver and the other passengers. I saw her head toss back in a playful, flirtatious laugh as they gestured her toward the car. My hand instinctively reached for the phone. Thankfully Doug answered quickly. "Come home immediately," I said emphatically. "It looks like Kalyn's going to try to leave our house with some kids who appear to be trouble!"

I knew that he could be home in less than five minutes as his office was just about a mile down the road, but I wasn't sure I had five minutes. I began to pray and cry out to the

Lord for help. I commanded the forces of darkness off of my property. I prayed for the protection of the blood of Jesus to descend upon my daughter and my home. Then I glanced out the window. I knew instinctively this could be a major turning point in our battle for Kalyn—either toward life or toward destruction.

Soon I watched Kalyn walk through the front door. "Mom," she said rather flippantly, "these kids want me to go with them for a while. I'm going, okay?"

Right then and there I knew what the enemy was up to. Our parental authority and leadership would be again directly challenged, and my role was already cast in this scene. At that moment I hated my part to play for I knew there would be a new season of persecution unleashed by my decision. But what else could I possibly do? My voice was surprisingly low and steady. "No, Kalyn, honey, you can't go," I calmly responded.

Almost immediately, as those words left my mouth, Doug's car pulled into the driveway and blocked the visiting car. I saw him head toward the driver's window as I watched the stormy anger rise upon my daughter's face.

"You never let me do anything!" she yelled as she stormed back out the door. I wasn't sure what was going to happen next in this pivotal moment. Would Kalyn yield to my command or defy me and return to the car and drive away?

I was amazed when almost immediately the car started its engine. Kalyn's quick response to the driver and Doug's presence in the driveway were transforming the scene very quickly. The car was leaving, Kalyn was crying and running to her room, and I stood at the window horrified, crying, and relieved. That day's battle with evil had been won.

That day in July became a showdown day in the Cherry home over the issue of parental authority. Similar kinds of horrible, torturous parenting scenes will be replayed in front yards all over America this week. I know because I hear about those scenes as I meet parents at churches, auditoriums, or shopping malls.

Sometimes the stories conclude as ours did—as narrow escapes from teenage disaster. More often, though, the stories conclude with sad, anxious parental reports of, "She wouldn't listen, and she went out anyway. Now we have even bigger problems." Or, more commonly, long, deep parental sighs are accompanied by negative headshakes and a resigned conclusion, "Well, she's sixteen, which is getting very close to eighteen. What could I say to her? I had to let her go and make her own decisions."

When I hear these words, I cringe. I recognize that my counsel to "just say *no!*" would not only be considered socially inappropriate but also outdated, insensitive, and perhaps even dangerous. And I certainly can understand why.

Most parents know about the "modern experts" who conclude that autonomous decision making and social independence are healthy needs and unquestionable rights of all modern teenagers and even younger children. We see their ideas reflected for us in the majority of TV sitcoms and movies we watch. We read about children's rights and emancipation of teenagers in court cases that are publicized.

But with such horrible difficulties and pains overtaking our current generation of teenagers, some foundational questions need to be asked: Who are these "experts" helping us raise our kids, and are we sure that their theories are correct? Where did they get their ideas? What if their theories are actually leaving our kids more vulnerable to predators and less able to receive our parental help and counsel? Are we sure that teenage rebellion is the developmental "norm" that we should, as parents, prepare ourselves to expect? Is it possible that we have been tricked into adopting a cultural mindset, which is actually damaging our ability to successfully lead our kids to maturity? Is it even possible that our own passive form of parental leadership is opening the door to disaster as we expect our children to make decisions that they are ill-equipped to handle?

Hold Up the Shield

Something deep inside of us wants to rise up and take charge of our wayward children. Perhaps that explains the attraction of television shows like *The Andy Griffith Show, Leave It to Beaver,* and *Father Knows Best.* These programs touch on some sort of God-given desire placed inside each of us to surround ourselves with more normal and healthy family role models. We may claim that Ward and June Cleaver's[1] style of no-nonsense home order would damage our modern, free-spirited prodigies, but inwardly we know better. The truth is, proper parental leadership, authority, and rules—mixed with obvious loving parental devotion to children—actually bring peace, order, protection, stability, and freedom to the next generation.

The pressures on our kids nowadays are part of a larger cultural phenomenon. Parents are entering a second reaping of the rebellious seeds sown in America and other parts of the world during the 1960s and '70s. Those years are commonly known as the era when Grandma's well-proven morals and values were tested and found to be too restrictive. "The establishment" was tested, and the rules were changed to become "less oppressive." In this current generational crop, however, the fruit of those seeds is not bearing well! While our kids' generation is wandering around in a humanistic pastureland of no moral absolutes, evolving truths, and free-love values, our generation must recognize that we're the ones who opened the gate to their pasture. We bought into the lies and the deceptions of a cultural shift that is threatening to collapse our modern families from the inside out.

We have dropped our shield of protection over our own children. Relativistic thought (truth is only true if I accept it for myself), pluralistic values (there is more than one truth), and evolving truths (truth is changing) have opened the door to this family governing system of anarchy, where each parent and each child constructs his or her own truth and rules his or her own self.

In this postmodern philosophical environment, "parental commands" by definition are reduced to a concept of "parental suggestions." When combined with the difficult pressures of broken homes, multiple parents, and blended-sibling groups, many are left in confusion wondering, "Who's in charge of this family anyway?"

Who *Is* in Charge?

I remember when Nathan and Kalyn were little and I was the new mom combing the modern parenting literature. I felt pressured to give them as much autonomy and decision-making room as I could, lest they be limited in their cognitive or social development. And while I secretly held disdain for those mothers who couldn't figure out how to appropriately give their young children free choice in the cereal aisle and also avoid a loud ruckus, I was convinced that my sweet innocent little Nathan could handle the cereal decision with only gentle mothering suggestions by me. For the most part, he generally did—but then came baby number 2: Kalyn.

Kalyn was so much more like her mother—more opinionated and vocal. After a few tries down the cereal aisle with my daughter, I immediately began to suspect that my mothering-by-gentle-suggestions leadership style might not make it through the next eighteen years with her! From the onset of those first baby steps, she seemed to be asking that normal childhood question that Nathan rarely asked, "Mom, who's in charge here anyway?" I found myself ill-equipped to answer her question. Confusion, frustration, and motherhood stress were the result. Thank God, He didn't leave me in such a bewildered state.

It was in this season of life that God broke through to my heart and set me free from so many of my spiritual deceptions. As He opened my eyes to the truth and accuracy of His Word, I discovered how my feministic and humanistic philosophies were directly impacting my children and my marriage. I realized that my foundational beliefs were actually blocking God's blessings in my family's life. So day by day He began to teach me from His Word about His principles of authority and leadership. Surprisingly, what He taught looked nothing like what I was experiencing in the world around me.

I had discounted all the Bible scriptures relating to the concept of "headship" or "authority" or that nasty "s" word— "submission." After all, wasn't this twentieth-century America, the land of the free and the home of the equal?

That is why it was such a shock to Doug when I approached him with the news that I wanted to submit to his leadership as the head of our household. "Head of our household?" he must of thought. "There's no such thing. We've always had two heads!" God had convicted me of my antiauthority and rebellious attitudes toward His ways that were so deeply ingrained in my postmodern mindset.

I remember quoting Ephesians 5:22, which says, "*Wives, submit to your husbands as to the Lord,*" and finally understanding it. God was doing a big work in my heart as He restructured my whole worldview. Something amazingly beautiful happened in our home as we embraced the simple truth of His Word. I was to submit to Doug as the head of our home. He was to love me as Christ loved the church. Our children were to honor and obey us as the God-ordained leaders of their lives. Suddenly a new peace and a new order settled into our marriage and our home. Joy replaced our striving with each other, and God's sweet presence flowed through our household decisions.

How I deeply regret we did not arrive at these truths years sooner. I know in my heart that some of Kalyn's struggles in her adolescence were probably due to my rebellion to God's ways in her early life. I regret that she didn't get from her dad or me the training in obedience she needed during her first six years. A wise teacher once taught me that the struggles with authority not conquered in toddlerhood become the struggles revisited in adolescence. I believe that to be true. Nevertheless, I rejoice that God's Word and His training deposited into her life during her middle childhood years eventually bore rich fruit, as promised in Proverbs 22:6: *"Train a child in the way he should go, and when he is old he will not turn from it."* Ultimately God's principles proved victorious in Kalyn's heart and mind.

> A wise teacher once taught me that the struggles with authority not conquered in toddlerhood become the struggles revisited in adolescence.

God's School of Obedience

This issue of authority is paramount in rescuing this generation from disaster. Our households must pass successfully through God's school on this issue. His system is not some optional plan we can opt out of if it doesn't suit our fancy. It is *truth,* and truth doesn't change.

It seems our parental challenge with the issue of rebellion is like the proverbial question, "Which came first, the chicken or the egg?" Rebellion to our parental authority can cause kids to fall into dangerous hands. But sexual wounds, abuses, and other secret soul damages are proven causes of rebellion in our kids also. So we feel helpless when we as parents are unable to help a child who simply will not listen to and receive our counsel. Meanwhile, our enemy just laughs.

Never was this pressure more vivid to me than when I stood in a hallway last year talking with a precious Christian mother about her son. It seemed her fifteen-year-old had become romantically entangled with a young teen girl he knew from his class. And soon the girl's mother began seeking out special attention from the fifteen-year-old boy as well. Obsessive text messaging, unusual "chance" meetings, and sudden volunteer work in the boy's classroom by the girl's mom led this mother into deep concern. Since she knew of our family's encounter with a sexual predator, she sought me out for personal counsel. My advice to her was clear and precise: "*Get your son away from this woman and run!*" I said with a kind yet firm tone.

I explained my concerns to the mom (of the son), and she readily agreed with my advice. This mother of her son's girl-friend was displaying many classic warning signs of sexual predatory behavior, which will be explained in further detail in chapter 11. But while the mother of the son shook her head in agreement, her face contorted as if in pain. Tears streamed down her face as she responded, "But, Lisa, I can't tell my son no! I am afraid of what he will do! He might rebel and then what would happen?"

My heart broke for this woman's plight. "What would happen?" I played those words over in my mind. "What would happen if she didn't say no?" I queried.

Something was terribly wrong. Mom was afraid, disem-powered, and confused. And now when she needed her best parental "No!" to work, she was too weak to launch it forth.

What are we to do in the face of such madness? Predators know how to misuse their power and use our own authority against us. We must be stronger *spiritually* than they are!

Whether you are a parent or are raising children in another capacity (legal guardian or grandparent, for instance), you can check out your own progress in this area by answering these questions:

- If you have younger children, can you give them a direction and be relatively sure they will obey that direction the first time without complaining or delaying?

- If you have teenagers, does your firm but loving no change their direction, or does your no seem like only a suggestion blowing in the wind?

- If you are a wife, are you submitted to your husband's leadership?

- If you are a husband, are you obeying God's Word completely and sacrificially loving your wife?

Thank God my no to Kalyn that day in the driveway, though not graciously received by an angry teenager, did succeed in stopping her behavior. Thank God Doug and I had enough restraint over her during those dangerous days that we could keep her safe when she was not emotionally or mentally capable of defending herself. Holding our place of leadership proved critical.

The issue of authority is amazingly intertwined with the issue of faith. Perhaps you remember the Roman centurion of Matthew 8 who was a Gentile, a person of a non-Jewish nation and faith. Yet when he faced an impossible situation with his servant, he believed that Jesus could give him a miracle:

> *A centurion came to [Jesus], asking for help. "Lord,"*
> *he said, "my servant lies at home paralyzed and in*
> *terrible suffering."*
> *Jesus said to him, "I will go and heal him."*
> *The centurion replied, "Lord, I do not deserve to*
> *have you come under my roof. But just say the word,*
> *and my servant will be healed. For I myself am a man*
> *under authority, with soldiers under me. I tell this one,*
> *'Go,' and he goes; and that one, 'Come,' and he comes.*
> *I say to my servant, 'Do this,' and he does it."*
> *When Jesus heard this, he was astonished and said*
> *to those following him, "I tell you the truth, I have not*
> *found anyone in Israel **with such great faith."**... Then*
> *Jesus said to the centurion, "Go! It will be done **just as***
> ***you believed it would."** And his servant was healed at*
> *that very hour.*
> —MATTHEW 8:5–10, 13 (EMPHASIS ADDED)

We see in verse 9 that the centurion understood authority and obedience. He believed in who Jesus was, and he knew that just as his own commands were obeyed, how much more would sickness and disease (and everything else) obey Jesus. As a result, he received his miracle from the Lord.

Our revelation of authority increases our capacity for receiving the promises of God for our children. We must believe Him and take Him at His Word. You may be thinking, "But I didn't start off on the right foot of obedience to proper authorities or to God." Let me encourage you that it is never too late to start passing God's school of obedience.

God's school is not like any other school system. He allows us to retake our tests until we pass! I'm living proof of that.

Perhaps you are a married woman and you have failed to honor your husband's authority in your home. You can repent and begin immediately. That is important because if we are planting seeds of rebellion toward our own husbands, we will undoubtedly reap on those seeds in the hearts of our own children. Yet we can stop this negative, spiritual process right now by repenting to the Lord. In time, our children will begin to follow our example. This is also true for men. If you are a husband and father who hasn't taken your proper place of authority as the head of the household and you haven't led your family in Christlike love to the truth of God's Word and His ways, you, too, can repent and begin a new path today.

If you as a parent, grandparent, or legal guardian have temporarily lost one of your children to the path of rebellion, you can begin to bring that child home through your prayers of repentance. Your repentance will open the doors for their deliverance!

Predators Understand Authority Too

This focus on the issue of authority and protection for our children could not be complete without addressing the misuse of authority by sexual predators. Abusers are masters at manipulation. Our children are vulnerable to confusion when the role of a potentially legitimate authority figure turns perverse. Obviously, teens and young children have a hard time resisting abuse when they are under the threat of being accused of disobedient behavior. Teachers, church leaders, older teens, babysitters, relatives, and even parents themselves could potentially capitalize on the "submission" teaching to their own perverse gain.

How, then, do we protect our children from the potential dangers of "blind obedience?" I think the key is in the word *blind*. Our children need to be discipled to recognize legitimate godly leadership. When they are equipped at home with correct revelation on proper obedience and honor, they are more equipped to recognize the counterfeit: abusive, blind manipulation. We need to teach them to realize that obedience to a higher authority may sometimes mean we say no to a lower authority. For instance, the command from a parent, "Do not be alone with an older man," is a higher level command than that of a teacher, older teen, or uncle commanding the child to join him in the bedroom.

But let's face it. These issues are incredibly tough for six-, eight-, or even fourteen-year-olds to grasp, let alone successfully manage. That is why you are reading this book. We, as adults, must take responsibility for every relationship into which we place our children. We must also take responsibility to train them, at whatever age they are now, to obey protective commands. Valuable resources to help are available at our website, Frontlinefamilies.org.

Staying in our position of authority takes courage, steadfastness, skill, and humility. We hope you will join with other Christian parents who are committed to standing against the cultural tide to train up a new generation of Christ followers. Our organization called POTTS (Parents of Teens and Tweens) can assist you. Through POTTS we can stand together in our local communities and our nation to raise up a new standard of hope for families. Go to POTTSgroup.com or follow the POTTS link on our main site, Frontlinefamilies.org. We will equip you with daily parenting tips, help you start a local POTTS ministry in your church, provide you with monthly video training, and equip you with resources you need to be successful.

God is raising up a standard against the enemy's best plans. Our job is to hear His voice, obey His Word, and prepare for battle.

Points to Ponder Chapter 6

- The issue of parental authority is a showdown issue of our day.

- Passive parental leadership can open the doors for predators.

- The erosion of absolute truth has led to the erosion of parental authority.

- Each child must pass God's "school of obedience" to successfully launch into adulthood.

- Child and teen rebellion today are both a cause and an effect of the problem of predators.

- Parental repentance of our own rebellion can open the door in the spirit realm for our kids' protection and healing.

Chapter 7

PREPARING FOR BATTLE

Battle Plan Steps 1–5

The wisdom of the prudent is to give thought to their ways.

—PROVERBS 14:8

About eighteen months had passed since our first night of crisis, and it seemed to me that so much had changed in our family. Gone were those days of subtle innocence—at least in my own mind. As I pondered how much the Lord had done to save our daughter and family from utter destruction, I was extremely grateful, but I was beginning to sense a new season was dawning. The pressure of those eighteen months was producing a smoldering passion on the inside of me to share with other parents the hope that we had found in our time of crisis and to see a generation rescued from destruction.

Although my confidence level of speaking to others was still shaken, I knew it was time to reach out and help those even in our own church who were in parenting struggles of their own. So one morning as I prepared to teach a Sunday school class, I grabbed a pen and paper to jot down a few notes about what I thought Doug and I had learned from our family's long ordeal. I was shocked when twelve important concepts that had become our "Battle Plan" emerged on my notepad. As I read that list, I was both comforted and saddened—comforted in the Lord's leadership during our time of crisis but saddened that many of our needed interventions had been delayed or flawed because we had not adequately prepared ourselves in advance of the battle. We made so many unnecessary errors!

My passion is for you, dear reader, to learn from our mistakes. As we move into the next section, we will be finishing our spiritual preparation for facing the predators. You will also learn how God delivered us the rest of the way out of our mess.

A healthy military consists of both a strong defense and a strong offense. It must be disciplined and prepared for the battles it may or may not ever fight. A healthy home is much the same. Normal parenting will produce its share of normal skirmishes that test our parental offensive and defensive responses. Over the next three chapters we will learn twelve keys that equip us for the minor battles, so we detect and circumvent the major predatory invasion. When not handled properly, minor battles can be *accidentally* escalated by parents into major battles!

If a parenting emergency/challenge hits your family tomorrow, are you prepared to skillfully respond? None of us can see ahead to our futures. But each of us can pull from the Lord enough wisdom and spiritual strength to face our future days in confidence. The next chapters are worth that investment for you. You will be ready to defeat even the predator's best shot.

The Five Steps of Battle Preparation

Step 1: STOP, Drop, and Pray

In the opening moments of a parenting crisis, are you more self-trained to go to the phone or to the throne? The Bible tells us the best thing to do first: *"In the day of my trouble I will call to you, for you will answer me"* (Ps. 86:7).

Times of crisis are times of intense mental, emotional, physical, and spiritual pressure. They almost always come by surprise, and so often that pressure will try to force us into an exaggerated sense of urgency that says, "I don't have time to pray about this. I must act *now*. I must say something *now*. I must stop this craziness *now*." In reality, however, most crisis scenes could be interrupted by at least a brief prayer

> Reckless words spoken can never be totally retrieved.

to allow God in on the problem. Sometimes refusing to respond to a situation on the spot, in the heat of the moment, is, in fact, your best hope as a parent. Reckless words spoken can never be totally retrieved and can sometimes cause a minor crisis to escalate into a megacrisis.

I've often wondered what the outcome would have been in our crisis if we would have paused our conversation after Kalyn stopped lying and finally admitted to the cell-phone bill. What if we had asked her to step outside our room for a few moments? We could have stopped and prayed for wisdom. We could have calmed our own emotions and received God's direction as to how to proceed with our conversation.

I know one thing for sure: God had a wise, grace-filled plan for how to respond to her humiliating disclosure. It was available from Him to us as parents, and I'm very sure that we didn't receive it. Instead, our own hasty, misinformed, reckless words pierced our daughter's heart like a sword. (Prov. 12:18.) What we needed were words seasoned with the grace of God. We needed words that would be *"apples of gold in settings of silver"* (Prov. 25:11), words that were totally appropriate to accomplish God's kingdom plan, set in a tone and atmosphere that was bathed in love and truth. Those kinds of words will not spill out from souls that are frantic, fearful, or undone.[1]

Although we responded wrongly to Kalyn, as soon as she left our room, we fell to our knees and began crying aloud to the Lord our words of desperate need: "God, help us! Have mercy on us, Jesus! What should we do, Lord? Oh God, save our daughter!" We knew He was our only hope. We also knew He alone could deliver us from evil.

Thank God we took our pain and voiced our cry to Him. We could have turned inward and sobbed, or we could have turned on each other in anger and cried out about each other's mistakes and weaknesses—but we knew better. We knew God alone would understand and hear our hearts' cries. He alone could bear our pain.

Throughout Scripture we find many cases of people who were in trouble and voiced aloud their needs to God. The children of Israel cried out during their slavery and were answered. (Ex. 2:23–24.) In the times of the Judges, the people would cry out to God for deliverance, and God would answer their cries. (Judg. 3:9; 4:3; 6:7–8.) Samuel cried out to the Lord when the Philistines were threatening to destroy Israel, and God routed the enemy. (1 Sam. 7:10.) But my favorite examples are in the book of Psalms. Psalm 142, for example, was written by David when he was in a cave hiding from his enemy:

> *I **cry aloud** to the LORD;*
> *I lift up my voice to the LORD for mercy.*
> *I **pour out** my complaint before him;*
> *before him I tell my trouble.*
> *When my spirit grows faint within me,*
> *it is you who know my way.*
> *In the path where I walk*
> *men have hidden a snare for me.*
> *Look to my right and see;*
> *no one is concerned for me.*
> *I have no refuge;*
> *no one cares for my life.*

I cry to you, O LORD;
 I say, "You are my refuge,
  my portion in the land of the living."
Listen to my cry,
 for I am in desperate need;
rescue me from those who pursue me,
 for they are too strong for me.
Set me free from my prison,
 that I may praise your name.
                         —PSALM 142:1–7 (EMPHASIS ADDED)

Crying aloud to God did not bring instantaneous relief to our pain, and we didn't just do it once on that night in October and never cry out again. But immediately, at the moment of our first cries, God's delivering hand began to work. He was now Lord over our situation. He was able to reach into our hearts to bring strength and hope and surround us with songs of deliverance. (Ps. 32:7.) He allowed our feet to hit the ground ready for the fight ahead.

Step 2: CALM Yourself in the Lord

Our praise and our worship of Him lift up His name above our situations and cause our souls to be quieted in His presence. When I was a child, one of my favorite hymns to sing was "My Hope Is Built,"[2] but it wasn't until recent years that I really understood the hymn writer's words: "When all around my soul gives way, He then is all my hope and stay."

A soul giving way is not a pretty sight. Emotions charge into overdrive and rational thinking goes by the wayside. King David knew how to control his soul in times of crisis, as he said, *"My soul, wait silently for God alone"* (Ps. 62:5 NKJV). Learning to control our souls is a matter of spiritual discipline. On a daily basis we have many opportunities to learn to quietly (or loudly!) address our souls. I like to practice this skill when the kids do irritating things like argue about the chores that have been their responsibility for five years or eat food in the upstairs living room, leaving their dishes for their toddler niece to spill. In the midst of any kind of turmoil, confusion, and pressure, we can say, "Soul, you wait in silence for God alone."

Our hope is based upon the promises of God, and He promised in Psalm 23 to be our good shepherd and to lead us "*beside quiet waters*" (v. 2). He promised to restore our souls, to bring them back to a place of order, rest, and peace. (v. 3.) He promised to prepare a table (a place of sustenance or feasting) before us even as our enemies are at work. (v. 5.) We can trust Him to do all of this as we claim His words of promise.

Calming yourself in the Lord is not just psychological relaxation. It is the action of receiving by faith the covenant promises of all He has purchased for us:

- His peace: "*The* LORD *gives strength to His people; the* LORD *blesses His people with peace*" (Ps. 29:11);

- His rest: "*He who dwells in the shelter of the Most High will rest in the shadow of the Almighty*" (Ps. 91:1);

- His strength: "*God is our refuge and strength, an ever-present help in trouble*" (Ps. 46:1);

- His might: "*You are the God who performs miracles; you display your power among the peoples*" (Ps. 77:14).

Those promises manifest in our lives as we meditate on and speak forth His Word. (Heb. 4:12). The Word of God is our offensive weapon. When all around our souls (our minds, wills, and emotions) are trying to give way, we need the Word to bring forth His promises and anchor our souls once again to the Rock.

What if during the heat of the battle, we can't even remember one Bible verse that applies to our situation? Thankfully, God has even provided for that:

> *In the same way, the Spirit helps us in our weakness. We do not know what we ought to pray for, but the Spirit himself intercedes for us with groans that words cannot express. And he who searches our hearts knows the mind of the Spirit, because the Spirit intercedes for the saints in accordance with God's will.*
>
> —ROMANS 8:26–27

Once our soul is restrained and quiet, God's mighty power working through our spirit can prepare us for the battle ahead.

Step 3: REFUSE Condemnation

Remember what we've learned—that when a parenting crisis strikes, our enemy, the devil, has by some method already attacked the child; the devil is now poised to push the parents into the dark night of the soul and then pull the parents toward the pit with their child. Yet his ploys can be foiled *by resisting his actions at the onset of the battle.* (See James 4:7.)

The devil's actions are revealed in verses that disclose his personal nature. In Revelation 12:10 he is known as the *"accuser of our brethren"* (NKJV). Another word for *accuse* is *condemn*, which accurately describes him because he's always trying to condemn us. Even when our own glaring parenting weaknesses and failures are screaming at us so loudly that we can hardly hear ourselves think, we must learn to boldly refuse all condemnation. It is paralyzing and does not come from God!

Condemnation is defined as "censure, blame."[3] It involves fault-finding, criticizing, and comes from the forces of darkness working on our own flesh. The condemning voice of our accuser is easy to recognize, as he speaks words like:

- "Your family is a failure."

- "You are no good."

- "You can't be a decent mother/father. Remember what you did?" (Or, "Remember what your mom/dad did?")

- "You always mess up."

- "God can't help people like you."

- "You're not going to make it through this."

- "This is all your fault. If you had just not done _____, then this never would have happened."

Scriptures describe the force of condemnation as "worldly sorrow." Second Corinthians 7:10 says, "*Worldly sorrow brings death*," but the same verse also says, "*Godly sorrow brings repentance that leads to salvation and leaves no regret.*" Notice, too, the words of hope in Romans 8:1–2: "*Therefore, there is now **no condemnation** for those who are in Christ Jesus, because through Christ Jesus the law of the Spirit of life set me free from the law of sin and death*" (emphasis added).

So we can resist the force of accusation and condemnation assailing our minds by saying *no* to those thoughts as they first pop into our heads and by absolutely *refusing* to allow our minds to dwell upon them.

Step 4: WELCOME Conviction

As we quickly say *no* to condemnation, we must immediately welcome godly conviction by saying *yes* to God. In the same way that worldly sorrow and wallowing in condemnation leads to death, godly sorrow and welcoming conviction leads to life. (2 Cor. 7:10.) *Conviction* can be defined as "the act of convincing a person of error or of compelling the admission of a truth."[4] To welcome conviction we must employ brokenness, truthfulness, and forgiveness.

"What happened to Kalyn wasn't fair!" I cried. I was a good mom doing good things for my child. I was a righteous woman living a clean and holy life. My mind tried to defend itself and reject the concept of brokenness and humility.

Only God knows the secret condition of our own human hearts. He knew that when we stood up to the voice of our accuser, the devil, we would attempt to defend ourselves and shout back at him, saying, "I am totally innocent of any wrongdoing," and then suddenly our own hearts would condemn us! What person can ever say that he or she is totally without any sinful motive, any sinful action, or any neglectful failure? How could we ever believe, think, or say we were perfect parents completely free of errors? So God allowed us an unpleasant but necessary journey into our own brokenness (or weakness).

I reluctantly had to face the fact that my personal weaknesses of pride, selfishness, and stubbornness had hurt my daughter and our relationship. I had sometimes allowed my sin to erect walls in our communication. Did my sin cause her destruction? No. Was I the one to blame for all of her great pain? No. Still, my sin was unmistakably intertwined in the whole painful mess.

Reluctantly, I had to face the fact that I had been inattentive to the warning signs of abuse that she was displaying (which we will tackle in chapter twelve). Partly, I was inattentive because I had acted in ignorance; partly I had ignored those warning signs because of my own pride and fear of man. I do not believe my sin directly caused Kalyn to be attacked and hurt, but it was a factor in the situation. Ignoring my sin didn't make it go away; justifying my sin didn't silence the devil's accusations of blame. Saying that my failures were only 5 or 10 or 20 percent of the problem didn't wipe away their significance.

My only real hope was to allow God's conviction full place in my heart. Only when I was truly broken because of *my* sin—not the sin of others—could I really cry out in repentance to the Lord and allow Him to cleanse me with His blood and then replace my weakness with His strength. (2 Cor. 12:9–10.)

From a posture of brokenness, we can cry out to God for His truth concerning our situation to be revealed. One of the Holy Spirit's jobs is to convict us of our sins. (Jn. 16:8.) So when we cry out to God, He answers by giving us His power and grace to receive the news of our sin. Then we can choose to repent of the sin that He reveals.

Many of us have never been taught how to properly repent of our sins. Perhaps we were raised in a home where the words, "I was wrong, I'm sorry," were rarely spoken. Or maybe we learned a shallow form of repentance that says, "Hey, if I did anything wrong, forgive me." Proper repentance is so much more. True repentance of our sin involves a three-step process:

1. we agree with God that what we did was sin and was wrong, and then we take responsibility for our actions;

2. we tell God we're sorry and ask Him to forgive us;

3. we turn away from our sin, forsake it, and begin to move our life in the proper direction.

As an example, let's say that during this time of crying out to God, the Lord convicted you of not spending enough time with your child. Perhaps He had previously warned you about selfishly pursuing your own personal hobbies at the expense of your family. Your time of repentance might sound something like this:

Lord, I agree that I have sinned. I was selfishly pursuing my own hobbies even when You warned me of my child's needs. What I did was foolish and rebellious. I was wrong to disobey You and leave my child open to the devil's attack. Please forgive me. Thank You that according to 1 John 1:9, You are faithful and just to forgive me of my sins and to cleanse me of all unrighteousness. Thank You that I am free from the power of that sin. (Rom. 6:14.) I turn from the sin of selfishness and disobedience. I give all of my life totally to You and ask You to direct all my ways, including how to use my time and effort.

> Our proper repentance will *open* the door to God and *close* the door to the devil.

Lord, take back the ground that I gave up over my child's life. Thank You for the power of the blood of Jesus that is delivering us from all the evil this sin allowed. I take my place of authority in the spirit realm right now and say yes to You, God. I say no to you, devil, and I disallow your activity in my household, in Jesus' name. Thank You, Lord, for Your good plans for us. Amen.

Our proper repentance will *open* the door to God and *close* the door to the devil. Then when the devil tries to stir in your mind the remembrance of your sin, you can remind him of your repentance and your Father's cleansing power.

These same three proper steps of repentance are also necessary to heal relationships that have been damaged by our sin.[5] Perhaps the Lord would convict you of specific sins you committed against your child or your spouse. If so, repent first to the Lord, but then also go to that loved one and repeat those same important three steps.

Step 5: DECLARE Your Promises

This is the step where we remind *ourselves* of all the good promises that God has made to us and to our family, and we put our spiritual weapon of the sword of the Spirit—the Word—into action to defeat the power of the devil's tactics. (Eph. 6:17.) God's Word is filled with wonderful promises that are made available to those who are in covenant relationship with Him (who have given their lives to Jesus and are, therefore, authorized to walk in His *exousia*). By some counts it is estimated that there are over six thousand statements of promise contained in the Word that are available to the child of God. Those promises cover every area of our families' lives—our *health* (Isa. 53:5; Jer. 30:17), our *peace* (Isa. 26:3; 54:13), our *safety* (Ps. 4:8; Prov. 1:33), our *deliverance* (Ps. 37:24; James 4:7), and our *provision* (Deut. 8:18; Phil. 4:19).

Speaking God's promises is how we declare our place of authority over our own lives. When we declare God's Word (His promises) out loud, it allows:

- our own faith in the Word to be increased (Rom. 10:17);

- God's Word to divide and separate truth from lies (Heb. 4:12);

- the release of the power of faith (Matt. 17:20);

- God's Word to defeat the power of darkness (Lk. 10:19);

- the power of the Holy Spirit to perform His own Word (Jer. 1:12).

If you have not yet discovered the power of speaking God's Word aloud over your own life and your own situation, I want to help you to learn more about it. I have a personal scripture declaration sheet that the Lord helped me write during our family's battle. It was so helpful to us then that I wouldn't dream of laying it aside now. If I go through all of them in a morning, it takes about fifteen minutes. You'll find my scripture prayer listed as Tool 1 under the section entitled, "Tools and Resources" on page 197.

As you make declaring scriptures an important part of each day, I believe you'll be amazed as you start seeing positive results in your life and family. This scriptural declaration not only transforms my mind and heals my emotions, it also transforms circumstances. I have watched God perform His Word so many times!

A few weeks after God gave me this scriptural prayer routine, I sensed His leading to do better at caring for my body during this season of intense stress. Months of overwhelming emotional trauma during my postpartum recovery from Lydia had left my body uncharacteristically weak. Though I've always exercised regularly, one day I decided to join a fitness center and distinctly sensed the Lord leading me to a specific one. I could get up early, leave the house and problems behind, speak God's Word during the twelve-minute drive there, do my thirty-minute workout, then finish speaking God's Word on the way home. The day He revealed that plan to me, I felt a new sense of hope. Getting out of the house three days a week would be worth the hour interruption of my morning routine.

My hope soon turned to anxiety, for when Kalyn heard about it, she begged to go along. Part of me was overjoyed that my depressed, lethargic, angry daughter wanted to exercise and even go with "mean old mom" to do it. But the other part of me screamed, "Oh no, it'll somehow be a mess. And I can't take any more mess!" So I told her rather emphatically, "If you go along, you'll have to drive (she had a permit), but there'll be no music or talking in the car. I'll be speaking my scriptures out loud all the way there and all the way back. So it won't be much fun for you. You'll have to sit in complete silence."

To my shock she responded, "Okay, I'll do that." I was shaken! How was I going to get my rejuvenating break now? But God had bigger plans than I did. He was busy performing His Word on our behalf, and I was so small-minded I couldn't see His plan at the time.

After a few weeks went by, Kalyn and I were both gaining physical strength, she was amazingly quiet and respectful of my scripture prayer routine, and I was rejoicing in some surprisingly positive mother/daughter bonding time. The crowning reward of our efforts came the day I accidentally forgot my Bible and scripture sheets. I was frustrated with myself yet determined to speak as much as I could by memory. That was the day when it dawned on me about God's bigger plan. As I stumbled to a halt with one of my scriptures, Kalyn immediately piped up and finished the verse for me. And all those weeks I thought she had been ignoring me! God got His powerful healing Word into Kalyn even when she was too weak or too defiant to do it herself. His Word would not and could not return void without accomplishing that for which it was sent. (Isa. 55:11.)

We get the power of God's Word working in our lives by asking the Lord to guide us to the scriptures specific for our situations and then personalizing them. For instance, we can pray and declare 2 Timothy 1:7 (NKJV) that says, "*God has not given us a spirit of fear, but of power and of love and of a sound mind*" by saying, "*I* was not given a spirit of fear, but *I* have a spirit of power and love and a sound mind."

If you are not sure you can believe the awesome good provision of God's promises that you are saying, that's all right! Just keep speaking those promises aloud and faith will supernaturally begin to rise up in your spirit, and you will begin to believe the Word. Our faith comes by hearing the message, and the message is heard through the Word of Christ. (Rom. 10:17.)

I once heard someone say that it is impossible to outthink the devil—but you can outtalk him! Jesus did that in His battle against Satan in the wilderness. Every time the devil brought Him a temptation, He responded aloud with, "It is written..." and then He spoke a verse from God's Word. (Lk. 4:1–13.) If Jesus needed to do this during His time on Earth to overcome the enemy, what makes us think we would need to do anything less?

Points to Ponder Chapter 7

- Parents need to be prepared with a spiritual battle plan in advance of any predatory invasion if they are to effectively destroy the enemy's plan.

- These twelve offensive steps in Chapters 7–9 can equip us to foil minor assaults before they escalate into disastrous attacks.

- Battle Plan Step 1: STOP, Drop, and Pray

- Battle Plan Step 2: CALM Yourself in the Lord

- Battle Plan Step 3: REFUSE Condemnation

- Battle Plan Step 4: WELCOME Conviction

- Battle Plan Step 5: DECLARE Your Promises

Chapter 8

BUILDING YOUR STRATEGY

Battle Plan Step 6

"Do not be afraid or discouraged because of this vast army. For the battle is not yours, but God's."
—2 CHRONICLES 20:15

The next step in the Battle Plan is powerfully illustrated in the story of Jehoshaphat, which unfolds with three enemy armies surrounding the land of Judah, poised to attack. King Jehoshaphat was very fearful and immediately sought the Lord and called for a nationwide fast. When all of Judah's inhabitants came together, Jehoshaphat stood in their midst and cried out to God. Then the Lord sent His answer to Jehoshaphat:

> The Spirit of the LORD came upon Jahaziel...a Levite...as he stood in the assembly. He said: "...This is what the LORD says to you: 'Do not be afraid or discouraged because of this vast army. For the battle is not yours, but God's. Tomorrow march down against them. They will be climbing up by the Pass of Ziz, and you will find them at the end of the gorge in the Desert of Jeruel. You will not have to fight this battle. Take up your positions; stand firm and see the deliverance the LORD will give you, O Judah and Jerusalem. Do not be afraid; do not be discouraged. Go out to face them tomorrow, and the LORD will be with you.'"
> —2 CHRONICLES 20:14–17

Notice that God spoke to His people and gave them a specific battle plan for their situation. They obeyed, sent forth praise and worship singers out ahead of the army (v. 21), and the Lord intervened. The enemies ended up destroying each other, and Jehoshaphat was victorious (v. 22). In that particular battle, the strategy was not to fight, but go down against the enemy, stand, and see the deliverance of the Lord. In other battles, God's strategies might look a little different.

Naaman was asked to dip in a dirty river seven times, and his leprosy was cured. (2 Kings 5:1–14.) Peter was asked to cast his net on the other side of the boat and his nets were filled to overflowing with fish. (Lk. 5:1–11.) Scripture is full of other instances when the Lord spoke to His people and gave them His plan—and He is still speaking to His people today. The captain of our salvation always has a plan. (Heb. 2:10 KJV.) The real question is, will anyone seek out His plan, listen to His instructions, and dare to obey them?

"He, who loved you unto death, is speaking to you," wrote Amy Carmichael, a well-known missionary to India for fifty-five years. "Listen, do not be deaf and blind to Him. And as you keep quiet and listen, you will know, deep down in your heart...." She revealed an important clue on hearing from God—keep quiet and listen.[1] That's a major part of Step 6. I know it was true from our crisis with Kalyn. Once I was able to get to a quiet place where I could hear God speak to my heart, it made all the difference between victory and defeat.

Step 6: RECEIVE Your Battle Strategy

It was December, two months into our crisis. When I look back, I see us all living in a strange thick fog. Kalyn was angry, mean, defiant, and hostile one minute and then weepy, sullen, and withdrawn the next. It was, to put it mildly, a mess.

After our first phone consultation with Focus on the Family's counselor, we had followed their advice and consulted a local Christian counselor. He was a wonderfully kind man who listened to our story and then worked with both Doug and me and then Kalyn. Yet somehow through that several-week process we made no progress, and he suggested we seek another solution. Kalyn refused to talk with him about anything deeper than the weather. She denied that anything at all had happened with the man, and she presented herself as a defiant teen in a stubborn state of rebellion. So for a very strange season of time, we were thrown off track and focused ourselves on getting help for a rebellious teen.

Looking back I can't understand why we didn't get some crisis help for the sexual abuse, but I have to remember how confusing our presentation appeared. Kalyn thought her problem was us and not the man; both she and the man denied anything sexual had taken place in their conversations; no one outside our family had witnessed all the ranges of her crazy behavior swings; and not many people are skilled at decoding the confusing aftermath of sexual-abuse trauma in a teen shrouded in the subsequent denial.

Some days I wondered if I could hold the house together at all. Each day I grasped for a new plan. How was I to care for a newborn, a toddler, two preschoolers, and five school-age kids—one of whom didn't have the will to live? Kalyn was losing weight at an alarming rate and looked horrible, so I'd let her eat anything she chose. She didn't come to family meals and lived in her room secluded, but at least once a day she would stomp down the hall to the kitchen, angrily grab a pan, shove it into the sink to fill it with water, and slam it onto the stovetop. If one of the other children stared at her theatrical macaroni-cooking sprees, she'd shout back angrily, "What are you staring at!"

After a few weeks of this strange madness, we felt led to reduce our potential areas of conflict to a bare minimum (for Kalyn's sake as well as the rest of us). We rearranged bedrooms to give Kalyn her own room, moved her daily schoolwork location to Doug's office, removed all family chores and baby-sitting responsibilities from her, and pulled her back from any outside-the-house job commitments like at church. Even then our lives were still a nightmare. I was in the full swing of the dark night of a mother's soul; Kalyn was in the pit; and unless we received a new strategy soon, Doug could see I was headed to the pit with her, a house full of kids in tow. So we made call after call looking for help.

It was Christmas break for school, and we knew we had to have a new school plan for Kalyn by January. We considered every available option—enroll her in a local private Christian school, sign her up for a public school, or send her to a boarding school for girls with behavioral problems. It is still shocking to me that we seriously considered that last option, but this way out seemed reasonable to me at the time! We still didn't really understand what our problem was, so our possible "solutions" seem rather ridiculous today in hindsight. *Me*, send my child to boarding school? I hadn't even sent her across town to kindergarten! But desperate times can sometimes cause us to reach for desperate answers. So Doug kept looking for an "out" for us.

> Desperate times can sometimes cause us to reach for desperate answers.

The Power of Seeking the Lord

We knew we only had a few days left to set up our school plan for the new year, but Doug wisely decided to send me on a little "relaxation" trip before we pressed through to make our decisions. I left the kids and Doug behind, packed my bags and the baby's bags, and headed up to the St. Louis area to check into the Drury Inn. I knew this was supposed to be a "vacation," but I had my own kind of "work" to do. I desperately needed to spend some time with my heavenly Father. On my way to the car, I grabbed my Bible and filled my bag with worship CDs and piles of Christian books from my shelves that I thought might contain some wisdom for the hour. I must have been quite a sight hauling all that stuff plus all my baby equipment through the hotel lobby!

Immediately I sensed the Lord's presence with me as I stepped into my car. In the privacy of my own vehicle and my own hotel room, my tears of pain flowed freely. But something was distinctly different about those tears. As they flowed out, rivers of God's healing love flowed in. For the first time in weeks, my soul was quieted enough to distinctively hear His still, small voice inside my heart. He strengthened me with His power and encouraged me with His hope. I heard His voice of instruction to abide in Him and rest as I read *Secrets of the Vine* by Bruce Wilkerson.[2] I felt my heart being filled with a new load of compassion for Kalyn and a new commitment to pray for her as I read *Rees Howells: Intercessor* by Norman Grubb.[3]

One night I stopped at a bookstore to do some research on teenage sexual abuse and was shocked by what I found. Although at that time Kalyn still adamantly denied that anything sexual in tone had occurred in those middle-of-the-night phone calls, I had never really believed her. Now I had the circumstantial evidence to suggest she might be lying. As I studied the literature, I was shocked to realize that Kalyn was indeed displaying classic post-abuse trauma symptoms. I knew that we had become so distracted and consumed by the tyranny of her urgent problems of rebellion and depression that we were being distracted from understanding the true root causes of these symptoms—the abuse.

I studied long enough to discover the magnitude of our problem, although I had to do quite a bit of digging. Literature on teen sexual abuse was much more difficult to find than literature on child sexual abuse, it turned out. I suppose this is understandable in an age when sexual scenes in the media and sexual experimentations among teens are considered common, if not normal. Nonetheless, I wanted to know how a mostly phone and Internet relationship could produce such damage. In order for what happened to truly be called "sexual abuse," wouldn't the man have had to physically touch her? When I read sections of Dr. Dan B. Allender's classic book on sexual abuse, *The Wounded Heart*, I finally began to understand the true nature of our battle.

> There is a deep reluctance to begin the process of change by admitting that damage has occurred...all inappropriate sexual contact is damaging and soul-distorting. Seventy-three percent of the least-severely abused victims report some damage, and 39 percent report considerable to extreme trauma as a result of past abuse....Verbal abuse is a powerful and deep wound. *Sexually abusive words produce the same damage as sexually abusive contact.* Yet the potential for minimization or feeling weird for being damaged makes the potential for change even more difficult for those more subtly abused than for those more severely abused.[4] (Emphasis added.)

(This made me realize that the destructive power of abusive words has strong implications for our era of social media!)

The author's words finally sank deep into my heart: our daughter had been sexually abused. Clearly, fourteen- and fifteen-year-old girls are not equipped to recognize and handle the psychological pressures of sexual predatory conduct, hence the breakdown in her behavior that we experienced. I was jolted to realize that instead of seeing my precious, bleeding daughter as a victim, I had begun to view her as a common juvenile delinquent, as evidenced by the disgust, scorn, disapproval, and anger I had felt toward her.

God was giving me a glimpse into a world I had never really understood before. I suddenly realized that many of those "repulsive juvenile delinquents" or impossible teens I had encountered were really like my own daughter—hard, rebellious, and difficult because they were covering up wounded, bleeding hearts. That day I knew it was time to shake off the dark night of my soul, roll up my sleeves, and get to work on the real frontline of this battle. Enough self-searching and analysis paralysis!

My journal writings of December 29 and 30 reflected my new understandings. I wrote, "The devil is the enemy—not Kalyn, not me, not Doug. The devil's trying to destroy us all in each of our areas of weakness—it's time to turn on him, not each other."

Then God did an amazing thing for me. He began to lay out a battle plan for the next season of our family's journey. His diagnosis and plan proved to be incredibly accurate. We have included my full journal entry on page 205 of this book. When I read it, I am still amazed at how precise God's diagnosis and prescription were for our family. But why should I be surprised? Whatever the enemy can cook up against our family or anyone else's, God always has the plan for our escape.

The Lord revealed to me that Kalyn's wound was like a cancer on her soul that had metastasized to all the other areas of her life. I realized that even if we had been able to cut off all the rebellious behaviors, get help for her depression, and reform her sensual behaviors, we still would not have healed the cancer. Our job was to protect her and love her while He worked to bring her to the end of her false coping systems and healed her wounded heart. We would have to do some very hard things in disciplining her on the way to our miracle, but He would give us the grace to stand.

A new hope dawned in my soul. God truly did have our plan of escape marked out for us. He did know what we should do, and He did have the ability to break through my hysteria with His plan. How could I have ever doubted? The sexual abuse was at the foundation of our problem, but it was facilitated by an unchecked root of rebellion. We had become like Jehoshaphat when he was surrounded by enemy armies and learned the power of seeking the Lord for His battle plan.

Building a New Life

I knew that day when I drove home from my personal retreat that the next step in implementing our plan would not be easy. Keeping Kalyn at home and protecting her (cutting off the metastases of the cancer as had God said) seemed almost as impossible to me as marching around a tightly shut-up city like Jehoshaphat had been instructed to do! But I knew that I must obey God's plan. So when I got home, I reported my revelations to Doug. He agreed that we should continue to home school Kalyn; but then, desiring to protect me, he asked, "Are you sure you can do this?"

> At times the plan looked logical; at other times it didn't.

I knew God had deposited His grace in my heart as I heard myself answer, "Yes, with God's power."

So it went with every step of our battle plan. We asked God, we waited, we received, and then we obeyed Him. At times the plan looked logical; at other times it didn't. Sometimes my own anxiety would overtake me, and I would frantically cry out to Doug, "What are we going to do now?"

Wisely he would repeat his well-rehearsed speech: "We are going to ask the Lord for wisdom and do the very next thing He tells us to do."

Sometimes we followed our best "heartfelt" leading by faith, and sometimes God would supernaturally give us a word of wisdom—like the day when I was seeking the Lord once again for a personal counselor for Kalyn. I heard these words in my heart: "Joyce Meyer's *Emotional Healing Kit*."[5] I suddenly remembered that years prior I had heard of such a resource from Joyce Meyer's ministry. I was so excited to discover the kit still existed and contained twenty-three hours of Joyce's best teachings on emotional healing, including *Beauty for Ashes*. But how would I ever get Kalyn to listen? Immediately God answered me. I was still her teacher! This would be her required curriculum for her high school Bible course. Miraculously, what started as an assignment she was reluctant to begin became her lifeblood. She poured over those tapes by the hour until she began preaching their messages back to me!

God would graciously work to comfort us and confirm His voice of instruction, so it would be easier to obey. Sometimes the instruction we thought we were hearing did not line up with the popular advice we were receiving from friends, family, and even some professionals. In fact, I had to constantly remind myself that while all those people truly meant well and wanted to help and while their solutions might possibly have some credence, only Doug and I were anointed by God as Kalyn's parents to sort through the available options for the God-ordained kingdom plan.

I can remember the horrible process we went through even after I returned from my retreat and was doing my best to hear the voice of the Lord. Immediately we faced even more pressure to give in to Kalyn's demands to go to a regular school. Part of me still wanted to agree, but deep down, I had no peace about her going. Her ability to stay out of trouble and away from the wrong crowd was nonexistent. She was normally an A student, but her ability to concentrate and learn course content was now severely limited. I felt in my heart that if we were to let her go right then, she could be gone for life. But then my mind would scream, "What if I am not hearing God correctly?" You talk about a faith test!

So God in His mercy gave us another word of confirmation. Since we had been greatly helped in the first week of our crisis by calling Focus on the Family's counseling service, in desperation I decided to call them back. This time I briefly relayed our situation, our long-term need for a female professional counselor for Kalyn, and our current need for a schooling solution for her. The counselor's response shocked me.

That very kind man responded with an amazingly succinct, clear plan. He explained that he was very familiar with the dynamics of a home-schooling family. Since Kalyn's heart had been stolen away from her primary life support system (her parents) and her school peers (her brothers and sisters), sending her out now to another school system could be a big mistake. He ended his conversation with a very impassioned plea: "Ma'am, it sounds like your daughter desperately needs to get her heart back home before she can successfully launch out to a new group of peers. She needs her family's love, and it won't be easy. Have you considered that perhaps, for right now, you and your husband could be her best counselors?"

When I hung up the phone, I stood in holy awe. The counselor had just confirmed everything I felt the Lord had spoken for us to do. A deep peace hit my heart as tears flooded my eyes. "Yes, Lord, as hard as this seems to be, I will obey," I prayed.

When we told Kalyn about our decision, she responded by getting angry and running away. Well, God warned me it wouldn't be easy! Minutes stretched into hours, and we didn't know where she had gone. I willed myself to stand strong in faith and not to give way to panic. I knew my faith in God's direction was being tested, so I continued teaching the other children and waiting for her return. Just minutes before we were going to call the police, she turned up in the basement, cold and weepy from her day in the chilly January woods.

Looking back on that miserable day, I am in awe of God's amazing grace—His grace to give us an answer to a very difficult question; His grace that enabled us to hold firm to our decision when that decision was tested; His grace to enact a school plan with a miserably reluctant student. Yet, I am totally convinced that our act of obedience in keeping her home was a critical turning point in our battle. Her heart would return home—miraculously and in God's perfect timing. We needed God's specific plan for our specific needs, and He gave it to us.

You can be encouraged in the Lord that no matter what kind of battle you could ever face in your home, God has a plan for your victory. It will be unique and individual to your particular situation. It will be filled with wisdom and seasoned with His grace. And it will work!

Points to Ponder Chapter 8

- God always has a strategy for every battle His children face.

- We must seek out God's battle plan as Jehoshaphat did by listening to His instruction and obeying.

- Battle Plan Step 6: RECEIVE Your Battle Strategy

- God's plans are specific and accurate.

- We must be content to receive the plan one step at a time if that is how the Lord wills.

Chapter 9

FIGHTING TO WIN

Battle Plan Steps 7–12

Love never fails.

—1 CORINTHIANS 13:8

The unfolding of our parenting crisis exactly coincided with the same month that a door miraculously opened for our church to purchase a permanent building. Up to that point, we had rented meeting rooms for four years. I don't believe it was a coincidence that we were faced with a decision to bid on this building while I was deeply tempted to shut down the whole ministry.

It is important for us to realize that our earthly life battles are actually a picture of a greater battle being waged in the heavenlies: *"Our struggle is not against flesh and blood, but against the rulers, against the authorities, against the powers of this dark world and against the spiritual forces of evil in the heavenly realms"* (Eph. 6:12). Clearly, to win these battles we must incorporate into our lives the twelve steps I discovered during our crisis with Kalyn. So let's continue with the second half of this Battle Plan, starting with praying our way to victory.

Step 7: FIGHT on Your Knees and Act in Love

I have never considered myself to be a "prayer expert." Sometimes during the intensity of our struggles my own mind would scream, "You don't know how to pray right anyway!" But I knew that was a lie. Jesus left us a model for prayer in Matthew 6 in what is known as the Lord's Prayer, and the Holy Spirit has promised to lead us into effective prayer (Rom. 8:26). By these verses, we can know we are well equipped.

I can go into my room, close the door, cry out, weep, and ask, and God will always respond. I can boldly pray with my scripture promises and receive God's wisdom and power and know my covenant with Him will hold. That's what I call "fighting on your knees," but it requires a daily decision to do it.

There were days I spent some forceful times in prayer in my bedroom. Yet as I turned the doorknob to exit my room and reenter my family room, God would remind me (in my heart), "You've fought in prayer, now go act in love."

The kind of love He was talking about is the kind of love with which *He* loves. In the Greek language it is called *agape*, and it can be best understood as a spiritual force—a force of the kingdom of light that drives back the forces of darkness. It is the kind of love that offers the ultimate sacrifice. The apostle Paul helped us understand the power of the Father's love in this passage:

> Our heavenly Father's *agape* love never fails.

Love [agape[1]] is patient, love is kind. It does not envy, it does not boast, it is not proud. It is not rude, it is not self-seeking, it is not easily angered, it keeps no record of wrongs. Love does not delight in evil but rejoices with the truth. It always protects, always trusts, always hopes, always perseveres. Love never fails.

—1 Corinthians 13: 4–8

One of the best examples of the demonstration of that *agape* power in action is found in the parable of the prodigal son. (Lk. 15:11–32.) When the younger son was given his inheritance early by his father, the son dishonored his father by foolishly spending his fortune on wild living and sinful lusts. But the father stood by patiently until the son came to his senses, repented of his foolish ways, and returned to his father's house. Even when the son ran from him, the father never left his post of love! When his son returned, he lavished his love and forgiveness upon his wayward child. The father's *agape* love never failed. I, too, have discovered that our heavenly Father's *agape* love never fails.

I'll never forget another day several months into our family struggle. I was exhausted. Kalyn's irritable, rebellious behavior had the whole household in an uproar. For weeks I could sense the very frightening state of my own mother's heart. The stress, anger, and sorrow were just too much. Now even my memories of peaceful days spent with the precious little girl whom I had nursed, rocked, and laughed were beginning to fail me. I couldn't conjure any more sweet warm feelings of love and devotion for her. Maybe we had had one horrendous verbal encounter too many. I just remember running to my room, falling onto my bed, weeping, and crying out, "Lord, help me! I don't feel feelings of love anymore for my own daughter." I was terrified by my emotions. After all, what decent mother could ever lose her feelings of love for her own precious child!

Lying there in my awful, miserable state, I could feel my heavenly Father holding me gently in His arms (not physically, but in a spiritual sense). Then He spoke His clear, calm words of comfort to my heart. "You are going to witness something you've never really understood or needed before. You will see the power of My love operating through you. And My love never fails. It can't. It is not based on anything but Me."

So began my new journey of faith: Faith in a Father's love that could flow through me to my daughter. Faith in a love that wasn't based on anyone's cuteness or performance or feelings. Instead, I was to discover the powerful, miracle-working spiritual force called love that is based solely on a written promise by a covenant-keeping God—and the truth of His promise that His *agape* never fails.

In the midst of our family battle, my children desperately needed my reassuring hugs and kind words. Kalyn especially needed my smiles and my warm motherly words of encouragement. Doug was amazing at this strategy. I would watch him tell Kalyn a tough, loving no and go right on to say, "Honey, let's go get some ice cream. It'll be fun." Then he would reach out and hug her defiantly stiff body. He wouldn't let her go. He was going to fight on his knees and then act in love—and I chose to follow his lead.

Step 8: RECAPTURE Your Child's Heart

I am so grateful that years ago Doug and I had heard a powerful message from a man named Dr. S. M. Davis, who tells the story of a man who had nearly lost his son to rebellion. His message was titled, *How to Win the Heart of a Rebel.*[2] He talked about the radical measures that father used to win back his child's heart after losing it to teen influences. The father took a leave of absence from his job, put his son in the car with him, and headed on a cross-country trip. After weeks of constant togetherness with no other influential voices available, God mended their broken relationship and turned the heart of that father back to his son and the heart of the son back to the father. (See Mal. 4:6.)

Doug's immediate response to Kalyn's meltdown was so painful for me to hear. "I've lost her heart," he cried amidst sobs of pain. Having worked so hard to capture and hold Kalyn's heart throughout her childhood, I knew how deeply he felt the sting of those words. Doug had taught others so frequently on the vital importance of a father—and a mother—holding on to a child's heart until that heart is able to be transferred to the heavenly Father and to his or her life partner at marriage. And now Kalyn's heart had been stolen.

I felt the pain with him. But at the same time deep inside me I felt hope, for my husband had already decided before that day in October that he would *never* permanently lose one of his kids' hearts. So I knew the final chapter of our life story had not yet been written. Doug would do whatever it took to recapture her heart—extra phone calls, trips to the mall, little notes of encouragement, lunch dates, hugs, pats on the back, little "I'm thinking of you" prizes, hours of time together, and even a trip to Florida.

Doug had always been so close to his daughter that her rejecting looks, abrasive comments, and sullen silences were piercing to his heart. Still, he persevered day after day, week after week. She was worth the priority treatment. Even if it cost him in his career and finances, she was worth it. He would win her over to life by his persistent display of steadfastness and love, and at the same time he would tell her no when necessary. His love had to mirror the Father's perfectly balanced love: completely unconditional and completely just. Doug didn't always achieve his goals perfectly. Yet he continued day in and day out until God's principle of fighting on your knees and acting in love worked in our home. Eventually, his persistence and hard work paid off and he did recapture Kalyn's heart.

> We must go after their hearts *now*.

If we don't make the time, sacrifice the energy, and develop the priority to recapture our children's hearts, who or what will hold them? The media? The boyfriend? The mall? The predator? Where will their hearts' allegiances lead them? We must go after their hearts *now.*

Step 9: CELEBRATE All Victories

My mind held a secret fantasy that I wished would come to pass. I imagined Kalyn being like one of those amnesia victims sometimes portrayed in the movies. One day she would somehow snap to her senses, rush to my bedroom, and shout, "Mom, I can see it now! I can't believe I was so blinded. Will you help me get out of this mess?" Then our family would sit down together and joyfully celebrate the end of the battle.

My fantasy sometimes brought me comfort, but more frequently it only brought me more frustration. Instead of an instantaneous, miraculous breakthrough like I wanted, we had to learn to recognize and celebrate each piece of victory when it came. I have discovered since then that most of parenting is like this. Somehow we had to be content with our day-to-day progress without selling out short on our ultimate goal: complete restoration and complete deliverance. Then, during those times when we weren't experiencing progress, we had to hold on to our faith.

Sometimes we even experienced setbacks, like the day when we felt Kalyn had progressed to a point where we could release her to take an extra computer class at our local junior college. We stumbled through our day of school registration only to have Kalyn blow up at me when we got home, get on her bike, and run away. We hadn't seen that erratic behavior for months. I was tempted to cancel all plans of promotion for her indefinitely until I discovered that she had just that week noticed her own progress and decided to come off of her anti-depressant medication cold turkey—without consulting us or her doctor. A person can't just all of a sudden stop taking that kind of prescription medication without risking serious side effects, one of which is erratic behavior. So, we had to face the setback, draw courage from the Lord, and get back on our course to victory.

Step 10: Get Proper SUPPORT

God does not expect us as believers to live isolated lives, meeting life challenges and flying our missions solo. Although He expects us to be equipped (with the armor He's provided for us) to stand alone against all antichrist forces (Eph. 6:11–18), He calls us His body (the body of Christ, the church) and expects us to work together in unity. Paul makes this truth clear for us in his letter to the Corinthians.

> *Now the body is not made up of one part but of many.... If one part suffers, every part suffers with it; if one part is honored, every part rejoices with it. Now you are the body of Christ, and each one of you is a part of it.*
>
> —1 CORINTHIANS 12:14, 26–27

When the Cherry family fell into crisis, many within the body of believers expressed a desire to help us bear our burden. For those expressions of love, we are eternally grateful. Some of our closest family and friends offered practical help—casseroles, babysitting, notes of encouragement. Others offered spiritual help by praying for us and offering us words of insight and counsel. We were and are still deeply touched by their sincerity and steadfastness.

During that season I learned a lot about receiving and giving help in times of crisis. I learned that while a crisis increases our need for others, it can also decrease our willingness or ability to receive the help they offer. I know my own emotional turmoil caused me to want to run away from people and hide. I was confused, embarrassed, tormented with self-doubt, and overemotional. I was well aware that my perceptions were faulty, and I desperately didn't want to hurt anyone else out of my pain.

To make matters worse, I couldn't tell others what was really happening because Kalyn was incredibly embarrassed and volatile about her situation. So sometimes the help or advice offered was sincerely meant to help, but it would be way off base. At times the words, unbeknownst to the speaker, were actually used by the devil to bring further pain and condemnation to me because my inner state was one of continual condemnation. Consequently, I found myself "over-armored" to deflect what felt like hurtful words—and that can be a dangerous state for relationships.

Something else I quickly learned was the importance of evaluating all practical and spiritual help before I accepted it in my heart. Not everyone who offered to counsel or pray with Kalyn or us was appointed or anointed by God to do so. We had to learn to give those situations to the Lord and quickly receive His best wisdom for how to handle each one. I had to realize that while I desperately needed to let others pray for me, I was not obligated to receive all that they said as truth. God was very gracious to give me an inner witness to those ideas that did come from Him. (See Dan. 2:20–21.)

During our quest for help, we also had to learn the vital skill of evaluating the professional help we received. We consulted with many types of services by phone, but we actually made visits to three different professional counselors (before the Lord led *us* to be Kalyn's counselors). I believe all three of those counselors meant well in their desire to help us; yet, none of them proved to be *the* answer we were desperately searching for. We did find, however, that in each case we had to be willing to sort through the counsel given because each professional did offer pieces of the answers we needed.

It seemed as though we were trying to reconstruct a giant jigsaw puzzle that had been blown apart. We couldn't get the whole thing back together without being willing to receive the pieces back one at a time as the Lord made them available. We also had to reject the pieces that were offered but were not a part of our solution.

The first Christian counselor we visited, whom I talked about previously, very kindly listened to our story and brought reassurance to us that we had not totally blown it as parents. He had seen many kids go through serious adolescent crises and still come through to maturity. We needed his perspective to give us hope! Yet he wasn't able to help us diagnosis Kalyn's response to the sexual abuse or to unlock her state of denial. So his ability to help over the long haul was severely limited. The second counselor we visited was a nightmare experience.

A Horrifying Evaluation

One day a few months into Kalyn's crisis, I entered her room to check on her and found her in bed, depressed, with all the covers over her head. Lying on the floor beside her was a notebook titled, *When Kalyn Dies*. All that week, she constantly left that notebook out for us to see. Daily she made horrifyingly dark and frightening entries in her journal about her wish to die, as well as other warped emotions she felt toward us and the man.

Doug and I wrestled as to what to do. We began following up on counseling leads again to no avail and strongly considered taking her to the emergency room for a psychiatric screening. But we knew where that could end—the local psychiatric hospital for adolescents. We didn't want that, so we continued to make calls until a secular psychologist agreed to see us. We were grateful to get an emergency suicide evaluation before we had to suffer through the weekend afraid—but this turned out to be a horrible encounter.

We filled out the necessary forms; and after chatting with us briefly, the doctor sent us out to the waiting room while he talked alone with Kalyn. When he called us back in, he gave us his diagnosis: moderately severe clinical depression but no immediate threat of suicide. That was good news! The rest of his evaluation, however, was horrifying. He believed that Kalyn would likely remain in this depressed state until she was old enough to leave our house—that is unless we made some serious changes in our beliefs. He stated that we had cut her off from her favorite friendship and that the loss of that relationship plus our "oppressive home environment" was the source of her depression. It was crazy! This man seemed to agree with Kalyn's deception! No wonder she was smiling as we came in.

In shock, I questioned his response to this sordid relationship and his answer chilled me to the bone. He said that he would need more information before determining whether or not the relationship was a problem. He went on to say that he was confident that if we'd start to bring Kalyn to see him, his counsel could be of some help to her. I immediately wondered what kind of help this forty-something man could possibly have to offer, since he did not appear to have a problem with a forty-six-year-old being in a relationship with a fifteen-year-old! I had never faced such an urge to punch someone in the eye. Doug sensed my emotions and immediately stepped in. He politely but firmly told the counselor that we wouldn't be bringing Kalyn back. Then he calmly wrote our check and got us out of there.

Kalyn was mad at us for a new reason. She fumed at us all the way home in the car. She liked the counselor and his ideas and wanted to continue seeing him. To her we were bad parents because we wouldn't let her! While that counselor got inside Kalyn's head far enough to help us know that she really didn't have an active suicide plan, the visit cost us dearly in our credibility in Kalyn's eyes. Clearly, that counselor was not God's ordained plan for help!

Line Up with God's Strategy

Counselor number three was a skilled Christian counselor, who specialized in adolescent issues and came on high referral. He was horrified at counselor number two's conclusions and was eager to help us. He suggested we get a copy of *Yes, Your Teen Is Crazy* by Dr. Michael Bradley[3] right away. (This book sheds light on some of the latest research on adolescent brain development and can be very helpful to parents.) Although the book did not espouse Christian ideas, it did explain the reasoning and behaviors of a teen in crisis and really helped us to understand some of Kalyn's struggle.

This counselor did a good job of evaluating our situation, but once again some of his conclusions were off base. He counseled us to immediately get her on antidepressant medication, which we did, and that proved to be helpful. He also counseled us to enroll her in school and allow her to do more "new things" that she was expressing a desire to do. His conclusion was that her root issue was a case of teenage rebellion, so we should treat that first and then eventually work her out of her desire for the forty-six-year-old man. I could see that some of what he said was true. But he still didn't seem to understand anything about diagnosing the trauma resulting from the sexual abuse and how those symptoms would interact with her rebellion and depression issues. So we took what help we could gain from our visits and left the rest behind.

I'm not saying that I wouldn't recommend counseling when faced with a crisis. I've watched many people receive great help from it, and I have recommended it to others in need. Understand, however, that all counseling is not of equal value. We need to shop for help with discernment. Counseling from a Christian perspective that lines up with God's specific battle strategy for your particular battle can be a great tool.

I encourage anyone in a crisis to receive all the help that God has to offer. Let Him use His body of believers to bring you healing and hope; but have the courage to politely refuse the "help" that is not from Him, while still blessing those who offer it. When you are not sure which is which, trust Jesus to sort it out and show you. After all, He is the "Wonderful Counselor," according to Isaiah 9:6.

Step 11: Stay in Your Place of AUTHORITY

Parents should never be tricked into either laying down this responsibility and benefit or giving it away to another: *you have been given* authority *over* your *own children.*

Remember the Greek term *exousia* that we learned about in an earlier chapter? We saw that God gave Jesus authority (*exousia*) over the forces of darkness and that He has given that authority to us as His followers. We can now apply that word to the sacred charge we have as the parents of our children. Our children were not given by God to the United States government to train. Our children were not given to the church or to the school systems to raise. While we may choose to use schools and coaches and pastors and Sunday school workers to assist us in our job, the ultimate responsibility for their lives remains with us, the parents.

When attacks come against your home, take a stand by faith and pray like this:

No devil, you'll not have my children, or torment my children, or drag my children down a path of destruction. I have been given authority over them; and as long as they are in my household, I have authority over your plans against their lives. "As for me and my household, we will serve the LORD" (Josh. 24:15)!

God has told me in His Word that I have been given authority to tread upon snakes and scorpions and over all the power of the enemy. (Lk. 10:19.) He also said that whatever I loose (allow) on earth will be loosed (allowed) in heaven, and whatever I bind (disallow) on earth will be bound (disallowed) in heaven. (Matt. 18:18.) So devil, I'll let you know right now that I disallow rebellion over my household, for it is likened to the sin of witchcraft. (1 Sam. 15:23 NKJV.) I disallow pride and bitterness. I disallow sexual predators from coming near my children. I disallow acts of sinful rebellion such as alcohol, drugs, premarital sex, and violence. I disallow tormentors such as nightmares, depression, oppression, anxiety, and stress.

Regarding me and my household, I say no to the curse as written in Deuteronomy 28; but I say yes to You, God, and to Your Word. I say yes to submission to authority in my life and my children's lives. I say yes to obedience, and because of that I say yes to all the blessings of Deuteronomy 28. I say my kids are blessed. They are protected. They are fulfilling their God-given callings and destinies. They honor their mother and father and it goes well with them all the days of their lives. (Eph. 6:2–3.) I pray these things in Jesus' name. Amen.

As parents, we *can* say no! Our prayers and our authority have power in the spirit realm. Though we may not see our prayers answered instantly in the natural (physical) realm, they are at work in the spirit realm from the moment we make our requests and declarations. We must learn to use our position of authority now like never before!

As the battle rages over this generation, God is looking for parents who will continue to stand in their place even when times are tough. Many have been tricked by secular ideas and concepts into abdicating their authority. Then they wonder why their prayers seem ineffective. What *we* allow in our families God has no choice but to allow. If we allow rebellion, sin, or strife, He will allow us to make our own choice.

Never have I experienced such temptation to give in and compromise as during our battle for Kalyn. When she would dress in ways that were inappropriately seductive and alluring, how I wanted to ignore what I saw. Oh, how I wanted to avoid the conflict and change my standard of "truth." How I was tempted to soften my preaching on sin and change my parenting style. When I could clearly see that my daughter was rejecting God and His ways and turning toward the ways of darkness and of the world, my mind wanted to reduce the problem down to a more comfortable and manageable size. I wanted to rename the rebellion and hardheartedness as simply a temporary developmental stage she would grow out of. But I knew better than to give in. It would have meant giving away my authority.

In crises parents may be tempted to let someone else take their place: the counselor, doctor, teacher, friend, "experts," pastor, relative, or even the child. Remember, however, *no one* else can effectively take on your role. Only you are anointed by God to be Dad or Mom to your child.

Step 12: WALK in Faith and Patience

To be ready for any kind of challenge, we must *intentionally* grow our faith much like bodybuilders grow their muscles— by repetitive use against increasing resistance. Bodybuilders don't get strong by thinking about lifting weights; they get strong by actually lifting those weights! In the same way, Christians grow strong in faith by taking God's promises and applying their faith until those promises are made manifest in their lives.

It is absolutely critical to walk by faith if we are to receive the promises of God. Receiving from God by faith is not the same as just positive thinking or hopeful wishing. *Faith* is the spiritual force of believing and trusting in God, even in the face of contradictory circumstances. When properly exercised, according to Mark 11:22–24, faith can move mountains.

I like Joyce Meyer's commentary on these verses in her *Everyday Life Bible*:

> Usually when we have mountains in our lives we talk *about* them, but God's Word instructs us to talk *to* them, as we see in Mark 11:22–23....
>
> First of all, what do we say to the mountains in our lives? It is obvious that we should not hurl our will at them; we are to hurl God's will at them—and His will is His *Word*.
>
> Speaking the Word of God is powerful and absolutely necessary in conquering our mountains. However, it is only the beginning. Obedience is equally important. If a person thinks he can live in disobedience, but speak God's Word to his mountains and get results, he will be sadly disappointed, as Jesus clearly stated in this passage.[4]

So what exactly is Bible-believing faith? I think the *Amplified Bible* version of Hebrews 4:3 helps us to understand: "*We who have believed (**adhered to and trusted in and relied on God**) do enter that rest*" (emphasis added). True faith, then, is an adhering to, trusting in, and leaning upon God.

Notice the object of our faith is to be God—not our own faith. I'm reminded of this daily when I meditate on Psalm 91, which says in verse 4: "*He will cover you with his feathers, and under his wings you will find refuge; **his faithfulness** will be your shield and rampart*" (or protective barrier; emphasis added). God does the work, I do the trusting, the leaning, and the obeying; and "by faith" the promises of God are realized.

There are enemies of our faith, but it is not that hard to recognize these "faith robbers" when we understand that the opposite forces of faith are *fear, doubt*, and *unbelief*. When these three are eradicated from the believer's life, faith will flourish. We can't afford one day of fear regarding the threats against our kids.

Faith is a key ingredient to receiving God's promises, but faith alone will not be enough. Hebrews 6:11–12 warns us: "*We want each of you to show this same diligence to the very end, in order to make your hope sure. We do not want you to become lazy, but to imitate those who through **faith** and **patience** inherit what has been promised*" (emphasis added).

Patience must have its perfect work just as faith must have its perfect work. (James 1:4 KJV.) So we may have to wait for God's appointed timing. Not many of us enjoy waiting, but waiting patiently is exactly what God expects.

I believe that *patience* is the most often overlooked part of the Christian's armor. After we're instructed in the Word to put on the full armor of God (the belt of truth, the helmet of salvation, the breastplate of righteousness, the shoes of the preparation of the gospel of peace, the shield of faith, the sword of the Spirit, and prayer), then we are instructed to *stand* our ground and to *stand* firm. (Eph. 6:13–14.) In other words, we're to wait patiently while God is at work and never give up. In our battle during the crisis with Kalyn, we needed great faith and patience for our miracle to come! Standing is not always easy or fun! But by God's grace we can do it, and He will prove Himself faithful.

Doug and I found three types of parenting situations challenged our faith and patience the most during our parenting crisis: 1) outbursts of erratic human behavior; 2) long, complicated processes; and 3) incomplete results. As you read Kalyn's account of her remarkable road to healing, watch for those three as they threatened our stand of faith.

Do you now feel better equipped for a parenting emergency after reading the Twelve-step Parenting Battle Plan? Perhaps you are like me, and reviewing these principles on a regular basis would be helpful in staying continually prepared. For your convenience, the following page lists all twelve steps of the Battle Plan. Feel free to remove it to serve as a review and quick reminder when you need it.

(Note: these steps serve as our "points to ponder" for this chapter.)

TWELVE-STEP BATTLE PLAN

1. **STOP**, Drop, and Pray

2. **CALM** Yourself in the Lord

3. **REFUSE** Condemnation

4. **WELCOME** Conviction

5. **DECLARE** Your Promises

6. **RECEIVE** Your Battle Strategy

7. **FIGHT** on Your Knees and Act in Love

8. **RECAPTURE** Your Child's Heart

9. **CELEBRATE** All Victories

10. Get Proper **SUPPORT**

11. Stay in Your Place of **AUTHORITY**

12. **WALK** in Faith and Patience

Chapter 10

MY ROAD HOME

He lifted me out of the slimy pit, out of the mud and
mire; he set my feet on a rock.

—PSALM 40:2

It was a sunny day in July 2003, and I (Kalyn) had agreed to
have lunch with my dad. We had just ordered ice cream and
were sitting in the parking lot. These lunch outings with Dad
occurred periodically and usually ended in an explosive battle
of wills and emotions. This day, however, something was
different. Though I would never have offered it, something
inside of me had changed—and my dad stumbled upon it.

As we sat eating our ice cream, my dad cautiously asked (as
he had so many times before) how I was feeling about my relationship with this man. Usually, this was where the conversation would head south and our lunch would abruptly end with
me exploding in anger and retreating to my familiar state of
withdrawal. But to his shock and mine, I told him that what
had happened between the two of us was wrong and very
much worse than what he thought. I began to cry as the story
flowed out. I remember falling into my daddy's arms, broken
and begging for help. As I opened my heart to let the poisoned
lies out, something else much more powerful flowed in—the
heavenly Father's love.

I cannot say exactly what caused the change on that particular day; I only know that scales had fallen from my eyes. I

was finally seeing a tiny glimpse of truth after living so long in deception and lies. After months of defending the very man who had violated me, I agreed to file charges against him.

I can only attribute this shift to the power of God working in my life. Supernatural truth had come into my heart and shattered a wall of lies. For the first time I realized I had been used and tricked. I felt embarrassed and angry as the reality of the situation sank in. But now my anger was not fixed on my parents or God but rather on my perpetrator, as well as the real enemy behind it all—the devil himself. This day was the first of three major steps to my getting back home.

Depression, Rebellion, and Unhealthy Relationships

One could scarcely imagine the joy and celebration of my family following this first day of facing the truth; however, the road home had only just begun and the extent of the damage to my heart had not yet been discovered. Though one battle had been won, the war for my healing was far from over. Consistency was something that would not be seen in my life for almost two more years.

The next season of my life was filled with small victories and large setbacks. I remember countless places along the journey when I was tempted to give up. Feeling defeated and tired of fighting, I often wondered if true healing was even possible. These roller-coaster days were difficult for everyone. I felt so fragile, like at any moment the small shelter of recovery I had built might shatter and I would have to start over again.

Because of the wound resulting from the sexual abuse, many dark behaviors and patterns emerged in my life. They were ugly branches growing from an ugly root. The three primary outshoots of my pain were depression, rebellion, and wrong relationships.

Because I had experienced this deep trauma during the years of identity formation, I had built my identity around the relationship with the perpetrator. I failed to recognize that this had created a false sense of who I was, so I embraced depression, rebellion, and unhealthy relationships as simply a part of the real me. For a time, each of these ugly monsters mastered me and sometimes all of them at once.

Since I had faced the ugly reality of what had happened, I could no longer live in my fantasy world. Every day for months I awoke with a fresh reminder of this painful truth, and some days it seemed more than I could bear. I would sadly retreat once again to my room under deep covers of darkness in my bed. I struggled with a very hopeless view of life. Despite the fact that I had been on antidepressant medication for several months, a number of my days were still spent in desperate grief, wondering how I could go on.

As for the unhealthy relationships, I seemed to attract all sorts of dysfunctional boys. Wherever I was, I would gravitate toward the neediest, struggling guys in the crowd. It was as if I wore a sign advertising my vulnerability. Because I felt a desperate need for a man's love and attention, I welcomed any and every advance, even when they were overtly inappropriate and purely lustful.

> I did not recognize the danger of the rebellion I was choosing.

I did not recognize the danger of the rebellion I was choosing. I knew my parents loved me, but I viewed them as power hungry tyrants, intent on ruining my life. Though I believed that I was paving the way for a freer way of life through these expressions of rebelliousness, in reality, every time I used one of them, their dangerous hold on me grew.

From these challenges came other common behaviors and struggles associated with sexual abuse. I experimented with cutting, since I thought feeling pain on my body would distract me from my heart pain. I also developed an eating disorder, thinking I could achieve worth to others and control of my life if I could weigh less. I thought I was the only one struggling with these worthless feelings. From discussions with countless teens facing similar crises since then, I now know how common these destructive coping patterns are.

Roller-Coaster Recovery

Though still struggling on many fronts, I experienced a second explosion of truth that was a milestone on my road home. It was November, one year after my meltdown. I had become involved with a wrong crowd of people who were masquerading as Christian teens. I was quickly being pulled down a path of more compromise and sure destruction. After finding myself in a very foolish and dangerous position, I awoke to the truth of what I was doing. I began to feel true conviction and a desire for change.

Once again I can only attribute this shift to the awesome power of a merciful God. I began to spend more time with godly people and thus began to be influenced by godliness. I am so thankful for the Father's timely intervention. Psalm 138:7 says, *"Though I walk in the midst of trouble, you preserve my life... with your right hand you save me."* God had spared my life again. After this second breakthrough, I began to experience more small victories, though setbacks still came. But God had a plan for my healing, and it would not fail.

I began to contemplate what I should do with my life after high school graduation. Deep down I wanted my life to count for something greater than me. Through a series of events that I can only attribute to God, I heard about a one-year ministry internship through Teen Mania Ministries called the Honor Academy, which was offered to high-school graduates.

This program consisted of Bible classes, mission experiences, intense discipleship, and hard work in an assigned ministry department. I did not think much about the Honor Academy until my parents suggested it would be a good option for me after I graduated.

Though not usually one to agree with their ideas, the opportunity to get out of town and do some good for others sounded attractive to me. But as I began to consider going, it seemed as if the enemy unleashed all of his best struggles for me, and my whole senior year turned into an intense battle for my future.

The roller-coaster ride of recovery was intensified in my life. I functioned quite well for periods of time only to take a dramatic crash right into the same rocks that I had visited so many times before: rebellion, anger, rejection, depression, hopelessness, and faulty relationships. I had been on this road of recovery for over a year now and was becoming frustrated that I couldn't reach a place of freedom.

The abuse I suffered had produced many attitudes, thought patterns, and identities that were foreign to the pure, God-loving girl I had once been. It wasn't until I was ready and willing to let God's deep healing work into my life that I found lasting victory.

Despite the constant struggles, progress was being made. Through Joyce Meyer's teaching tapes and books, powerful truth was being planted in my heart. But even more significantly, God was miraculously paving the way for me to be placed in an environment where He could get through to my heart. Though deeply entangled in an emotional relationship with a young man from our church, warring with my parents on seemingly every decision, struggling to discover who I really was, and fighting to be in charge of my own life, I felt God impress something on my heart that I could not ignore.

I knew beyond any doubt that I had heard God's voice even in the midst of turmoil, confusion, heartache, and weakness. He told me if I would act on His leadership and go to the Honor Academy, He would sort out everything back home. At that time, this sounded like a pretty good deal. Though I was rejecting most of what God was trying to get through to me, I somehow grabbed hold of this one promise with child-like faith.

At the same time God was working, the enemy tried to pull me into erratic, bizarre behaviors to keep me from the destination God had for me. When I say bizarre, I mean bizarre! Like the day that I got mad, threw a golf ball through my window, and used the glass to cut my arms and legs. My parents were freaked out! But God's hand was still at work, preserving my life and leading me on. Despite the intense opposition, I made it to my internship program. I knew that God had a purpose for me there, and I settled in, choosing to simply trust. Little did I know that my life was about to be turned upside down.

Final Breakthrough Day

February 10, over two years after my meltdown, is a day I will always treasure as the final breakthrough day. On this ordinary Thursday, I encountered the living, holy, all-powerful creator of the universe. My life would never be the same again.

Five weeks into my Honor Academy internship was a scheduled fasting and prayer retreat—a two-and-one-half-day fast from food and talking. This time was to be spent seeking hard after Jesus. I was scared. I was still clinging to *my* way of doing things, *my* plans for my future, *my* control of my life. Yet I had a sinking feeling that everything was about to change.

At the opening ceremony, the lights were dimmed and worship music filled the room as six hundred people cried out to God. Suddenly, it was as if everything around me ceased. I felt His presence so strong that I became unaware of my surroundings. There were no people; there was no music; it was only my heavenly Father and me—the Father that I had rejected, hardened my heart to, and run from. That night my Father called me back to Himself. I began to break on the inside as the creator of the universe spoke clearly to me, revealing the wickedness of my own heart.

The words God spoke were heavy words of warning and truth. He showed me I was a rebel in my heart, despite my outward service to my parents and Him. He was giving me a period of grace where I could choose to turn. If I did not change, I would die. Words cannot describe the severity of God's words in my heart. I was faced with a choice, yet it did not feel like a choice at all. I became keenly aware that I was a prodigal and it was time to return home. The power and presence of God were so strong that as soon as I cried out yes, I literally began to be transformed from the inside out.

> As I reached the end of myself, I found the beginning of God's supernatural power.

As I lay on the hard floor of the auditorium, I wept in realization of my hard heart. I experienced heartfelt repentance for my sin and received the indescribable mercy and forgiveness of the Savior. As I reached the end of myself, I found the beginning of God's supernatural power. I had come home to my Father, surrendered to His will for my life, and established Him as *my* Lord.

God uprooted many of my faulty foundations, cleansed my heart, and set me on the path of life. As I began to see Scripture in truth, light was shed on my ways of darkness. Through the book of Proverbs, God showed me I was the rebel and harlot Scripture warns about. God also lifted my eyes to see the future He was calling me to—a life of freedom, purpose, and kingdom work. Excitement took over as I considered what my life could hold when I was completely surrendered to Him.

The freedom I had been searching for, fighting for, and begging for was finally mine. It came through the doors of brokenness and radical submission. I was now ready for true restoration and healing.

Immediately after the retreat, I took action. Through tears of joy, I called my parents to share what God had done in my life. I asked their forgiveness and told them I wanted to come home and rebuild. I had many other things to make right as well. No matter how difficult some of these were, they were all done with new purpose and new joy because I was walking in obedience to the new King and Lord of my life.

After years of shunning authorities whom God had placed in my path, I found myself thanking them. I thanked my parents for saying the no's that saved my life. I thanked my family for loving me when I was unlovable and thanked many others who had supported me in prayer through this difficult journey. Their faith had ushered in my breakthrough.

This turning point made way for true progress in many areas of my life. First, my relationship with God became real. I entered into an intimacy with Jesus that I had scarcely imagined possible. As I spent time with the Lord daily, His Word came alive in my heart. A passion for holiness and truth and a desperation for God's presence caused me to dig deep into the things of God. Second, I became strong enough to face the abuse that had happened to me. God used my experiences at the Honor Academy to lay a foundation upon which He could bring me true healing. Third, God brought restoration within my family. The months and years of hardness, anger, and cruelty toward them had created a large chasm of hurt between me and my parents and siblings. I had a passionate desire to see restoration come into each and every relationship.

I can vividly remember the shock of my family and friends when I came home from the Honor Academy in Texas. I was no longer the hardheaded, mean girl who had left just a short time before. God's supernatural love had overtaken me, and it held the power to restore broken relationships. I had a desire to serve and love my parents and siblings like never before. I realized how much I had taken for granted, and I desperately wanted my place to be restored within the family. I allowed them to become my support system like they had always wanted to be. The times that I spent with my family became treasures to me, and I thank God continually for their place in my life.

God had proven Himself victorious over the enemy's attacks, over pain, and over sin. At the same time, He was preparing me for the finishing processes of healing I would still walk through.

The Trial

During my last semester at the Honor Academy, two-and-a-half years after filing charges against the man who had abused me, we found out that our case was going to trial. I took two weeks of emergency leave from the academy and flew home to testify in court.

Shortly after beginning the process, I understood why so few victims of sexual crimes choose to press charges. The grueling, embarrassing, drawn-out court proceedings were an experience I would wish upon no one. It was undoubtedly the most difficult thing I have ever walked through. I knew God held my heart, but I still felt afraid. Often during those two weeks I contemplated quitting the process. I sensed the pull of depression and hopelessness knocking at my door and felt terrified that I was going back to the pit of despair. Yet God's grace was enough, and He pulled all of us through.

The jury found the man guilty of aggravated criminal sexual assault—specifically, indecent solicitation of a minor. I remember the indescribable relief I felt when the verdict was read and the trial was over. After still struggling with feelings of blame and responsibility over the relationship, it was extremely helpful for my healing to realize that I had been a victim. The abuse I experienced was not my fault, and the court system had proven this to me.

Though relieved, I felt beaten up by the whole process. Having to relive all of the events and face the man in court was very stressful. For several weeks I experienced symptoms of post-traumatic stress disorder, including nightmares, panic attacks, and depression; but through it all, the Lord upheld me. Day by day I pressed on, trusting God to pull me through.

Although I experienced much victory during this chapter of my life, it unfortunately ended in an unsettling way. Through an odd series of events at the sentencing hearing, the court case was sent back to the judge. The defendant, my abuser, had hired some new lawyers who had found a technical loop hole in the original court proceeding. After a two-year appeal process in the appellate court, the case was ordered back to the local court and the state's attorney never enacted a retrial. Sadly the judicial system left the case unfinished; nonetheless, it was closed in my heart. I made the conscious decision to forgive this man and release the situation to God. While it is very unfortunate that this man is free, did not face consequences for his illegal actions, or become registered on the sexual offenders list, I know we did our job to report what had happened. I chose to walk free and start the new life God had for me.

A Work in Progress

My road home could be described as many things—long, hard, trying, challenging, but also victorious! I can appreciate the joys and struggles along the way, for I can see how God used what the enemy meant for evil in my life and turned it into something good. I now claim Psalm 40:1–3 (NASB) as my life verse.

> *I waited patiently for the* LORD*;*
> *And He inclined to me and heard my cry.*
> *He brought me up out of the pit of destruction, out of*
>   *the miry clay,*
> *And He set my feet upon a rock making my footsteps*
>   *firm.*
> *He put a new song in my mouth, a song of praise to*
>   *our God;*
> ***Many will see and fear***
> ***And will trust in the*** LORD (emphasis added).

God pulled me out of an impossible pit, cleaned me up, and gave me a reason to live! I can look back through the years and chuckle, realizing sometimes in humorous terms just how far God has brought me. Yet I also recognize with seriousness just how far God still wants to take me. I welcome His work in my life and desire that He form and fashion me just like the potter fashions the clay. (Isa. 29:16.)

Joining the Front Lines

Sadly, my story is not uncommon. The enemy is picking off young people left and right through the hands of predators. Sexual perversion, abuse, rebellion, depression, suicide, drugs, alcohol, eating disorders, and self-mutilation run rampant today. Don't be naive and ignore the symptoms. There is truly a battle raging for the hearts and minds of this present generation. I have felt the pain of being on the losing side of the war. I have also heard the stories of countless children, teens, and parents who are facing the pain of destruction by evil intruders. At the same time, I have seen the redemptive power of our God. He has a deliverance plan for all who will run to Him.

Now is the time to rise up and to take your place in the battle for your kids, your family, and this generation. I am committed to fight for righteousness and truth. We must join the front lines.

God put a passion in my heart to carry His message of hope to the world. After graduating from the Honor Academy, I moved back home to be part of the amazing family God gave me and to be involved in the ministry work He called us to. I found God to be faithful once again as I continued to grow and trust God with my future.

After completing my degree in social work, I started working closely in our church's REALITY youth ministry. Opportunities began to arise for me to share my story with others caught in confusion and pain. Truly God is using what the devil meant for evil to bring about His healing power. God also restored my dreams. After a beautiful courtship, my dad walked me down the aisle to the most amazing man in the world. Adam and I founded our relationship on the kingdom assignment God has for us, and we love serving in ministry together. Our beautiful baby girl, Kyla, is teaching us the wonderful joys and awesome responsibilities of new parenting, and we are taking our place on the front line to protect her.

I now know for a fact that nothing is impossible with God. No situation is too hopeless, no heart is too hard, and no pain is too deep that our God cannot heal. He is all-powerful, and He is able to bring a miracle when one is desperately needed.

So, if you find yourself simply observing the crisis of others or you are alone in a crisis yourself, sinking in a pit or traveling a road of restoration, I encourage you to press on. Don't quit fighting and don't give up—don't give up on yourself; don't give up on your loved one. Yet more importantly, don't give up on your God! One day you will be on the other side of the story and your eyes will be opened to the greatness, the power, and the mercy of our great God. He is faithful!

Points to Ponder Chapter 10

- Truth sets captives free!

- Some battles experience setbacks before ultimate victory results.

- We, as parents, must remain calm and faithful as we lead our children.

- No problem is too complex for the Lord.

- He can turn our greatest test into a testimony of His power.

Chapter 11

SEXUAL ABUSE 101

The discerning heart seeks knowledge.
—Proverbs 15:14

Over the years many have asked Doug and me if we had warning signs of the predator's activity. That's one of my most torturing questions. Since hindsight is always twenty-twenty, it is still hard for me to second guess. Surely there were clues we did not notice, and I suppose we will never know what they were. But for educational purposes, let's look at what I do know we missed.

Some eighteen months before our meltdown...

Kalyn seemed to develop a crush on the twenty-one-year-old son of the family friends whose husband and father would abuse her. The crush was nothing serious. The young man was a fine upstanding Christian, who never acted on Kalyn's slightly giddy response to his presence. She began primping before every music practice that his family would attend with our family. I chalked it up to normal young-teen infatuation.

Some thirteen months before our meltdown ...

Kalyn would pull away from Doug's normal, healthy, fatherly displays of affection such as arm pats or quick hugs. She would put her arm up as if to say, "Don't come too near." Having always been a daddy's girl, it was quite a change. "But," we would sigh, "she is growing up!"

Some one year before our meltdown ...

Nathan and I joked about how Kalyn would do anything to help the father (and even sometimes the mother) of the boy she had a crush on. She carried his equipment, defended his musical ideas in our worship-ministry practice, and treated him with extra kindness. I assumed it was a transferal of interest to the whole family of the boy whom she "liked."

Some nine months before our meltdown ...

Kalyn asked for a webcam for a Christmas present. It was not an unusual request as it was the hot new technology toy of that year. She and Nathan figured out how to use it by consulting our family friend (the abuser) who was a technological genius.

Some ten months before our meltdown...

Doug received a phone call from a coworker of the perpetrator, who was also a mutual friend of ours from church. While at work, he had seen the man chatting online with Kalyn, and he was concerned about her. I remember the very strange basement meeting we had with Kalyn concerning the warning phone call. Her behavior was so odd and out of character. She was defensive of the perpetrator and strangely angry about her dad's order for her to cut off all contact with him immediately. I remember the strange darkness that fell over her face for a few seconds. I had never witnessed that dark look before and wasn't to see it again until that dreadful day in October.

I remember leaving the basement and meeting with Doug in our bedroom. I was strangely shaken by our conversation, so I asked him, "What was that all about?" But I don't remember us concluding that we needed to investigate further, and I don't remember ever really questioning Kalyn's answers. After all, she had never lied to us before. We were confident she would obey our order to stay clear of the man whom we no longer trusted.

Some six months before our meltdown...

We discovered that the family friend (the abuser) from our church was involved in an online relationship with a woman after his own marriage had recently collapsed. Doug went to him and warned him about his online behavior, suspecting the man had fallen into online pornography also. Doug, as his pastor, rebuked him sharply, even mentioning the scripture about how it would be better to have a millstone tied around a man's neck and for him to be cast into the sea than to cause one of His little ones to stumble. (Lk. 17:2.) He did not talk with him about Kalyn, as it appeared she was obeying our warnings to steer clear of this man we now labeled as dangerous. Although the man was traveling nearly fulltime on business at that time, we rarely saw him at church, but when we did see him, we kept him at arm's distance.

Two-and-a-half months before our meltdown ...

I asked Kalyn about her recent weight loss. Increased exercise and a reduction of junk food was her answer. "Don't you think I look good?" was her question to me. It was logical, so I didn't think anything more of it.

Six weeks before our meltdown ...

I caught Kalyn coming out of the garage (where many of the damaging phone calls occurred) after having her "quiet time," as she called it. Concerned about her choice of clothing, I stopped her on the front sidewalk and said, "Honey, that is not an acceptable outfit. Why are you wearing that?" I remember the strange look on her face when I questioned her about her sudden change of wardrobe. I couldn't put my finger on what exactly was different, but in recent weeks she had begun suddenly demonstrating a more seductive look.

One month before our meltdown ...

I noticed Kalyn would frequently fall asleep in the afternoon. I just assumed it was a need for extra adolescent sleep.

Three weeks before our meltdown ...

Kalyn was an absolute delight to be around. She was extremely chatty with me, offering to do extra chores, performing her schoolwork with excellence, and managing her teen emotions with amazing maturity. I remember asking Doug, "Does it seem to you as if Kalyn has suddenly aged several years all at once?" We chuckled and delighted in the "progress."

Two weeks before our meltdown ...

Kalyn walked into the kitchen and leaned her fifteen-year-old elbows on the counter in a thoughtful way.

"Mom, I am just so much more comfortable with adults these days than I am with kids my age. People my age are just sooooo immature!" I remember smiling to myself with delight at her mature observation not realizing she was "age progressing" herself to make sense of the perverted relationship.

In Retrospect

Listing this timeline now makes me feel like a total fool. How could we not have seen our problem? We saw the smoke, but we didn't look hard enough to find the fire—and we didn't know what the fire looked like when we did see it!

I was equipped to detect spinal meningitis symptoms in my kids but was totally ill equipped to detect symptoms of sexual abuse. Why? It couldn't have been that I wasn't smart enough to understand it. I am a very educated woman. Or so I thought. My problem was lack of knowledge combined with a perceived sense of insulation. Bottom line—I did not believe that it could or would happen to us; therefore, by very definition I was totally ignorant of sexual abuse.

That is why I have titled this chapter "Sexual Abuse 101." I do not want any other parent to be ill equipped and vulnerable as I was. If we had been spiritually prepared as we have discussed in earlier chapters and practically equipped as we will discuss in this and the next chapter, we could have prevented our problem. That, my friend, should be enough motivation for you to read on!

Please do not consider this primer an all-inclusive guide. Remember this is course level 101. I encourage you to use it as a springboard for continuing education. I will give you the foundation on several key concepts all parents and church leaders must know. On our website, Frontlinefamilies.org, we provide excellent website links and updated resources for your follow-up education.

Eleven Definitions for Understanding Sexual Abuse

We will explore the complex issues related to sexual predatory behavior by focusing our learning on the meanings of ten key terms. A working knowledge of each should produce a protective base for you to successfully lead your family.

> Abuse can be classified under two main categories: *contact* and *interactions*.

1. Sexual Abuse

"Sexual abuse is any contact or interaction (visual, verbal, or psychological) between a child/adolescent and an adult when the child/adolescent is being used for the sexual stimulation of the perpetrator or another person."[1]

Before this happened to us, I believed abuse had to involve physical contact of some kind. However, abuse can be classified under two main categories: *contact* and *interactions*. The concept of *contact* can include fondling, kissing, oral sex, or intercourse. Fully clothed touching would also be included.

Interactions can be quite varied but would include sexual solicitation or verbal fantasizing as well as virtual descriptions of sexual practices and terms. These interactions can occur in person or via phone or media connections. Visual exposure of a child to pornographic imagery, sexual acts, or sexual body parts is also abusive.

Psychological sexual abuse occurs when relationship boundaries are crossed or privacy issues are violated. Adults should not use a child as a surrogate spouse or have an intrusive interest in a child's developing body. Cases where fathers repeatedly enter a closed bathroom door to view a girl's body or cases where mothers are lying around naked in front of teenage boys produce relationship violations that damage.[2]

Abuse can be understood as *ab*, which means "away from," plus *use*.[3] When anything is used away from the way God designed, problems result.

2. Child Sexual Abuse Victim

Victims can be infants, toddlers, children, or adolescents from every walk of life. The exact number of victims is unknown; however, experts estimate that 1 in 4 girls and 1 in 6 boys are abused in some form by age 18.[4]

Abuse is *never* the fault of the victim. Even if victims put themselves in a position of risk due to wrong choices, abuse is the responsibility of the abuser. Victims will need help placing the responsibility of the abuse on the correct party.

Children do not seduce adults.[5] All sexual behavior between a child and an adult is the responsibility of the adult. Because of this legal and moral responsibility, minors are not held legally liable for sexual relationships until the state-determined age of accountability. About half of the states set the age of consent for sex at 16 with the other states naming 17 or 18 the legal age.[6] These limits—set by law—are designed to protect adolescents, yet many groups including the homosexual lobby want to see the age lowered.

Preteens and teens make up a large portion of victims; however, societal views of adolescent victims are very complicated. Because of the sexualization of our culture, most adults and teens have a hard time viewing teens as victims. We have been conditioned to see them as sexually active and cognitively mature, so we wrongly assume they can defend themselves.[7]

Victims often experience a "freezing" response in their bodies during the abuse, so it is highly unlikely they will fight back. Since God intended sexual nerve endings to produce feelings of pleasure, the combination of fear, violation, excitement, and pleasure is extremely confusing for the abused.[8]

3. Sexual Abuse Trauma

God never intended a child to be involved in any type of adult sexual activity, so when an adolescent or young child is violated, abnormalities will follow. Some victims (and even victims' families) may develop post-traumatic stress, which is a mental health disorder. All victims will develop coping methods to deal with the inner pain of violation. Most develop some form of denial mechanism to attempt to minimize the conflict. Issues of anger, perceived powerlessness, inner contempt, betrayal, and ambivalence can produce rebellion, withdrawal, depression, sexual immoralities, eating disorders, substance abuses, self-mutilation, and a host of other problems. [9]

The trauma has both short- and long-term effects. Seeking treatment and healing for the wound as quickly as possible after the trauma is highly advantageous. Sexual abuse wounds left hidden, resurface in victims' lives—often in their own marriage and parenting experiences. Jesus has healing for all complex soul wounds! Seeking help from qualified sources can speed that healing. See our website, Frontlinefamilies.org, for resources and referrals for help.

4. Grooming

Grooming is a term used in psychological, mental health, and law enforcement circles that describes the conniving manipulations the sexual perpetrator uses on his/her victim. If it were easy for victims—or the professionals and loved ones surrounding them—to detect the manipulative deceptions of abusers, we would not need this book.

Usually molesters work hard to earn the trust of the adults surrounding their victims before they attack the children. They may appear so helpful and so outstanding in kindness that even when warning signs are present as to their activity, adults dismiss the evidence in their own minds as ridiculous. That helps explain why a teacher, coach, or pastor can keep this activity below the radar for so long. As adults, we like to believe we are good judges of character, so when evidence to the contrary surfaces, we often suppress it quickly as it can feel like a place of vulnerability.[10]

I could not have understood this unless I lived it myself. Even in the face of the evidence before us, it was incredibly difficult for me to reconcile the fact that the man—who at one time had been a trusted friend—was a molester. I just did not want to believe it. Perhaps it was my own form of denial to insulate me from my own form of violation.

Grooming behaviors toward victims will often include subtle threats of harm to the child, the child's family, or the offender. The child is given the responsibility to keep the secret and is often manipulated by bribes. Perpetrators usually groom the child to receive more and more overtly sexual behavior by starting with minor violations first. Complimenting achievements becomes compliments over physical features, which becomes touching of or exploitation of body parts—usually with the child's passive participation.[11]

5. Pedophile

The term *pedophile* is derived from the psychosexual disorder, *pedophilia*, which is identified in the official diagnostic manual for mental health professionals called the *DSM-IV-TR*, the *Diagnostic and Statistical Manual of Mental Disorders, 4th edition, Text Revision*. The technical diagnosis of someone being a pedophile would require the presence of several characteristics, including "recurrent, intense, *and* sexually arousing fantasies, urges, *or* behaviors involving prepubescent children, generally age 13 or younger."[12]

In popular use, we interchange this word with the terms *child molester* or *sexual offender*. However, it is important for us to understand and differentiate the terms.

True pedophiles tend to have a lifetime pattern of attraction to children with a preference for children as sexual partners, but they may and often do have sex with adults too. They will often position themselves strategically in close proximity to their victims by volunteering or working in environments with children or adolescents. They are opportunistically helpful: volunteering to babysit for the worn-out single mom, helping with after-school practices, cleaning up after the child birthday party, driving the teen home from the club meeting. They are truly acting as the nice guy or girl. Rarely do they present as the stereotypical scary man in a trench coat. Pedophiles can leave a trail of a large number of victims numbering into the dozens or hundreds.[13]

6. Child Molesters

A *child molester* can be defined as a "significantly older individual who engages in any type of sexual activity with individuals legally defined as children."[14] Child molesters can be male or female, single or repeat offenders, or violent or nonviolent in their behaviors.

Their victims can be infants up to adolescents who are legally still considered children. The term "significantly older" is generally recognized as being a five-year age difference. Older adolescents can fall under this distinction of child molester if the behavior fits the power-abuse dynamic generally represented in the five-year distinction. Thirty-four percent of child sexual abuse is perpetrated by a juvenile.[15]

The terms *child molester* and seem to be used synonymously. Abusers do not fit a stereotype. They represent all age, educational, religious, racial, ethnic, socioeconomic, and social backgrounds. Molesters can be single or married, male or female, heterosexual or homosexual.[16]

Unlike pedophiles who are overtly attracted to children, many molesters are more situational. These are men or women who, under certain stressful conditions in the adult world, "go down" to the child or adolescent world to find "sexual success." Or they simply may be acting on a moral indiscrimination or impulse. Some of these individuals are like big kids who never seem to grow up—at least in some areas of their lives. Others can morph into other forms of abuse (like elder abuse) when their situations change. Often pornography is involved with the behavior.[17]

> Over 90 percent of the time the abuser is known to the victim and/or the victim's family.

Over 90 percent of the time the abuser is known to the victim and/or the victim's family. Approximately 39 percent of molesters are family members with 56 percent estimated to be acquaintances of the child or family. The younger the victim the greater the chance of the offender being a family member or juvenile. [18]

Family structure has been found in a recent study to greatly influence the risk for sexual abuse on children. Children living with two biological parents are at lowest risk. Risks increases for children with single parents or stepparents. The risk for children living with a single parent cohabiting with an unmarried partner is *20 times* higher than a child living with two biological parents.[19]

The above facts should greatly affect our parenting decisions, which we will explore in the next chapter.

7. Sexual Assault

The term *sexual assault* is the new terminology used in law enforcement for rape. As its purpose was to expand the concept of rape to include males also, its definition is much broader than our traditional use of the term *rape*. In many states the wide range of behaviors we discussed under sexual abuse, including sodomy and molestation, would be a form of sexual assault.

The risk for sexual assault continues beyond the age of eighteen for our kids. Any forced sexual behavior imposed on another person is illegal. Ninety-two percent of rapes and sexual assault victims in 2005 were female with sixteen- to nineteen-year-olds in the age group at highest risk. However, only 39 percent of rapes or sexual assaults are ever reported, making it one of the most underreported crimes. Males are the least likely to report.[20]

8. Abuse Disclosure

We should not expect our children to automatically disclose these kinds of problems, even if we have a close relationship with them. Since 73 percent of victims do not tell anyone about the abuse for at least a year[21] and 45 percent of victims not telling for at least five years, we could be fooled.[22]

Telling the secret violates all denial mechanisms working to protect the inner world of the victim. The perceived threat from the abuser and potential blame of the victim also strongly deter disclosures to trusted authorities. If kids do tell, many will choose a friend over an adult to disclose to.[23]

Being emotional and spiritually ready to hear of a problem is vital for parents. The opening moments of disclosure are critical for the victim. *Never, ever* blame your child, even if you can see some foolish things that he or she did in the situation.

9. Abuse Detection

To *detect* is "to discover the existence of."[24] Once sexual abuse has occurred, we hope to quickly detect it so all wrong behaviors can be stopped and healing can begin. Unfortunately detection is not easy since we cannot count on overt disclosures.

Young children through teens who have been abused will experience a wide and varying list of possible side effects, including but not limited to: nightmares, withdrawal, pseudo-maturity, running away, sexual or seductive behaviors, early promiscuity, loss or increase in appetite, change in school behavior or performance, physical symptoms in the genitals, reluctance to go certain places or see certain people, defensive behavior toward the abuser, outbursts of anger, crying spells, head or stomach aches.[25] (For more information, go to Frontlinefamilies.com)

That is an overwhelming list of possibilities! Especially when it is combined with the other coping strategies of teen problems we talked about under "sexual abuse trauma" above. Here is a critical observation: since many of the cases of abuse remain unreported for years, parents and youth workers will often only discover the abuse by digging deeper into the roots behind other serious teen issues. I have personally heard so many disclosures from teens (and adults) presenting with other needs like promiscuity, problems with pornography, substance abuses, eating disorders, cutting, depression, or rebellion issues that I have now made it a practice to screen for abuse in every case I can! If it is there, healing for secondary symptoms will be dependent on healing the abuse wound.

Becoming skilled at recognizing the warning signs for common teen challenges as listed above is important for today's parents. Adolescent depression, for instance, can be easily confused for other behavioral issues. We have excellent tools on our website to help you increase your ability to screen for problems.

10. Reporting

Once a case of sexual molestation has been detected, it always raises the question of who should be told. Many professionals such as teachers, nurses, doctors, pastors, social workers, and counselors are considered mandated reporters by law. In other words, they are expected to inform the authorities of their suspicions of abuse, even if they do not have conclusive physical evidence.

Reporting is usually made to two systems that work together in each state: the local law enforcement and the local child protective agencies. After a report is made to law enforcement, the chances of arrest and prosecution are quite low. After analyzing the research estimates from agency and government sources of reporting, arresting, prosecuting, and sentencing rates, a leading educational and advocacy group for sexual abuse prevention, Darkness 2 Light, states, "Assuming that all research and data presented is valid, logic suggests that substantially less than 3 percent of child sexual abuse perpetrators serve jail time."[26] While the registered sexual offenders lists maintained by the state can be computer accessed by lay people to help us screen our acquaintances, the chances of an offender making the list is very slight.

Some might wonder why anyone would bother to report offenses with these discouraging statistics. However, reporting illegal activity is our civil responsibility. I will say that how, when, and where to report predatory behaviors requires the wisdom of the Lord as we will discuss in the next chapter.

Become familiar with your local authorities and systems of help. In our case, we were very cautious about jumping into any system that we felt could work to confuse or hurt our daughter further. As Christian parents, it is vital to choose help wisely and never yield your place of leadership over your own child or family.

11. Abuse Prevention

To *prevent* something is to keep that event from occurring. Obviously, that is our number-one goal for our children regarding any form of abuse. Child abuse awareness programs in the past have made serious errors in focus related to prevention. Let this next statement sink into your mind deeply to help counteract the past misconceptions: *sexual abuse prevention is the responsibility of the adult—not the child.*

As the adult, it is my job to supervise every moment of my children's lives. If I entrust one of my children to another, I still remain responsible. I am responsible to detect and remove potentially dangerous situations from my child's life. I am the one who can be equipped to recognize and avert problems.

My children should be taught safety principles, *but* my children by very definition cannot be equipped to protect themselves. Teaching my children about good touch/bad touch is not true prevention. If they have experienced bad touch, they have already been abused. Good touch/bad touch has more to do with early detection. We must go deeper with our family's prevention plans.

We have seen most of these key terms related to sexual predators exemplified in our family's story. Now that we have built both a spiritual and natural understanding of this key issue for our homes, we will cover *Twenty-Six Tips for Sexual Abuse Prevention* in the next chapter.

Points to Ponder Chapter 11

- Learning about sexual abuse makes it less likely that a predator can stay hidden in our midst.

- Sexual interactions of any type can damage our kids.

- Molesters work hard to earn the trust of adults.

- Our greatest threat from predators comes from people we know rather than strangers.

- Many sexual abuse cases are only discovered because of the dysfunctional side effects.

- We cannot rely on law enforcement to keep our families safe from predators.

- Sexual abuse prevention is the responsibility of parents and adults not children and teens.

Chapter 12

TWENTY-SIX KEYS FOR PROTECTING YOUR CHILD FROM SEXUAL PREDATORS

Discretion will protect you, and understanding will guard you.

—PROVERBS 2:11

After the attack on Kalyn, I was tempted to withdraw my family from all of society. But, of course, that was not the answer to protection! Instead I realized I needed to courageously face the predatory forces that have penetrated our society and shifted our environment. We may say to our children, "Follow God's plan for your life, and stay clear of the dangerous traps that could ensnare your heart and defraud your soul." But if they naively ask, "What traps?" we know we have a great deal of parental work to do. Now that we have unmasked both the spiritual and natural characteristics of sexual predators, it is time to conclude our study with twenty-six practical things we can do to protect our kids.

Sometimes people ask me what I do differently to protect my children now. My list below is my best answer to that question. After identifying the common deceptions that attempt to infiltrate our minds, refocusing our homes on the absolute truth of God's kingdom, and taking our place of parental authority, we can trust the Lord for the wisdom and grace to guard our kids.

Many of these keys to protection need to be studied and developed further than what I can survey for you here. As you read the list, ask the Lord to lead you to the keys that are most important for your family right now. You can find follow-up material to assist you at Frontlinefamilies.org.

The Twenty-Six Keys

1. Understand Developmental Vulnerabilities

When my children were babies and toddlers, I was constantly consulting growth and development charts to make sure they were on track and that we were meeting their needs. But it seemed once we entered the school years, I rarely consulted those developmental charts. Perhaps it seemed we had entered a quieter and less complicated season. And then adolescence hit, and we were scrambling for understanding again!

As we were recovering with Kalyn, I was saddened to realize I had not properly assessed her developmental vulnerabilities. I think the problem was deeper than a lack of knowledge about teens, for I had studied enough in college on the issues not to be able to claim ignorance. I think it was a case of thinking my child was not "typical." Maybe I thought she was advanced or maybe I thought she could intellectualize her way past her biological brain immaturities. Either way, I made some serious miscalculations that have sent me back to those growth and development charts for study.

Micah at fourteen has certain inner struggles that Ethan at eleven is not yet facing. I need to be ever mindful of that and asking, "How could the enemy work his plan most effectively against Micah right now? How could he capitalize on his immaturities and weaknesses?"

In my house, the challenge is that I also need to ask the same questions about Josiah who is five, and I will need to ask those same questions about every six months for all the others, too, in order to keep fresh on new growth stages. It is a big job but critical. Sometimes a quiet strategy session with the Lord with your Bible in one hand and the developmental charts in the other is the most effective plan.

2. Keep Your Mental Watch List

Since it is my responsibility to protect my children from those who would abuse or deceive them, it is my obligation to watch over every person in their lives. I no longer consider anyone above being watched. I do not expect to have problems from my closest family and friends, but I never allow myself to cross people off the list in my mind. Instead, I purpose to evaluate all data for any warning signs. This is not a posture of fearfulness or paranoia but rather leadership.

I enlist the help of others in my family (including my children) to report any suspicious concerns. This has led to many interesting observations. Most have been harmless, but over the years a few have warranted adjustments.

3. Limit Unsupervised Contact

Since over 80 percent of abuse cases stem from one-adult/one-child situations, reducing the amount of unsupervised one-on-one contact between my child and another adult or older teen can lower our risk.[1] *Unsupervised* means outside of public view. Privately talking to a child within a public room is less risky than talking with a child behind closed doors or in a car.

Places where your child is attending functions without you should purposely limit one-adult/one-child contact situations. Our website can link you to other wonderful sites that can help organizations maintain the highest standards of prevention. Compare those standards to your children's places of exposure to evaluate your family's safety.

4. Teach Your Kids

Our kids need to learn some of the very same things that we have learned in this book. Warn them of the tricky nature of deception. Lay a foundation of absolute truth. Teach them to fear—have a healthy respect for—the Lord. Help them understand that while God has a plan for their lives, the devil will also be attempting to work his plan. Equip them to discern light and darkness in the world around them. Explain the principles of authority and the concept of *exousia* and *dunamis*. In other words, follow the outline of this book. Start on the spiritual principles (even when they are too young to grasp all the concepts fully), and then build them toward an understanding of the natural world.

God's Word is filled with scripture about predators. It is a sex-education training manual and spiritual-warfare tactic book all wrapped into one! Study the fall of Samson, and don't just sugar coat the part about his hair. Read the book of Proverbs and learn the behaviors of the adulteress, the harlot, and the prostitute. Look together at what happened to David's family when a brother violated a sister and a son rebelled against the father. Unmask the predatory forces in the pages of His Word, and then go to Internet newsfeeds and continue the unmasking.

Next, you can use Kalyn's story to explain the sneaky tactics of a child molester. Read to your children the entrapping words used by the perpetrator. Role-play with each child the kind of tactics you could imagine would be most enticing to him or her. Investigate your children's personality and love languages,[2] so you can help them with their greatest areas of temptation. For instance, if your child's love language is "words of affirmation," flattery could become a real enticement. Teach your child how to recognize it by lavishing him or her with compliments, then teach the child how to fend off advances.

Teach them to confidently respond to anyone who tries to ask them to keep a secret, "I tell my mom and dad everything," which would likely send a molester running. Explain good touch and bad touch. Use correct names of body parts when explaining. Let them know they should always tell you if someone is acting odd and bothering them, but then give them the freedom to go to someone else to tell also. Remember, however, that in all your training you should never put absolute trust or reliance in your child's/teen's ability to comply. Fear is a lousy motivator for either our children or us. Demonstrate your confidence in God and then take your responsibility as the adult!

5. Provide Early Sex Education

Our children, from the time they are preschoolers, will receive sex education every time they go through the grocery-store checkout and nearly every time they see a TV commercial. Shouldn't *we* be the ones who intentionally teach them the foundations of sexuality? God's plan is beautiful. The world's is a cheap counterfeit. Because we are so oversexualized as a culture, our children will need more and earlier explanations than we are naturally comfortable with. That is an unfortunate reality that I cannot change. Our aim, however, should be to have our words echo louder in our children's ears than those of their friends or teen movie stars. Excellent materials are available to help us, but we must bravely take our place! See our resource suggestions at Frontlinefamilies.org.

6. Recognize the Fallacies of Early Maturity

As dedicated Christian parents, we have discipled our children in godly character and biblical standards. We have embraced a model of ministry that has always included our children ministering alongside us. Because of our intentional training and the grace of God, our kids have excelled in maturity compared to many of their peers. They are comfortable working alongside adults in the church and enjoy serving in leadership capacities at a young age.

Can you see where I am headed here? Early maturity is a great goal, but it caused some unique vulnerabilities for Kalyn. She was comfortable in the adult world, and others began to see her as older and more capable of adult reasoning than she actually was. Parents, some forms of wisdom only come from years of experience and observation. Never lose sight that your child, however mature, is still a child. Prematurely treating a child as an adult can be a symptom of your own parental pride. Challenge them to maturity, but recognize that children's brains—which are still forming in the adolescent years—are still capable of childish errors.

> Never lose sight that your child, however mature, is still a child.

7. Involve Extended Family

Protecting our children from predators should be a shared responsibility in an extended family system. Unfortunately, many extended families are broken and/or ill equipped to help provide protection. Some may even be your greatest areas of vulnerability. If possible, however, discuss the new things you have learned in this book with your extended family. Explain your family's safety policies, and ask their help in maintaining the "watch list." Do not expect grandparents from a previous generation to automatically understand some of the predatory deceptions of this era. Update them and ask for their prayerful assistance where possible. Draw strict lines denying *any* unsupervised contact with any family members known or suspected of displaying abusive behaviors. Your child's safety is more important than potentially hurting someone's feelings.

8. Hire Computer Accountability

Staying current with ever-expanding technologies is tough for today's parents. Personally, we are very conservative in our home with handheld devices of all kinds. Obviously they can draw our kids into a distant world with an almost hypnotic pull. Setting and readjusting family screen-time policies is a big ongoing project. Just when you settle into one system, somebody gets a new piece of equipment. It is our job, however, to always stay at the helm of the technology ship.

We need help with this task. That's why we hired an Internet accountability system called Covenant Eyes (see Frontlinefamilies.com) to watch over our home computers and provide us with constant parental continuing education. I love their system, which can block sights; but they take accountability to a new level by sending us a monthly report of every place our computers have attempted to search. Wow, has this raised the bar in our home! When Dad or Son or Daughter know that their other family members will see every search-word typed, it maintains a high wall of mutual accountability. We maintain access to everyone's computer and keep a close eye on any Internet activity; yet still we cannot let down our guard one minute!

Every family must make their own decisions on the issue of social networking. Personally, our teens are not allowed on facebook until they are out of high school. They have personal e-mail accounts and blogs, but we have not felt that facebook is a place we want them to be at these most vulnerable years. Chat rooms and skyping are not allowed. YouTube is a real challenge and must be monitored with close supervision. Any inappropriate YouTube searches would show on our Covenant Eyes.

All the greatest at-home systems are wonderful. But let's face it, computers are everywhere. Inspiring a heart of purity in our kids that transcends our rules and reach is the biggest hope—and that comes through the Holy Spirit's work in their hearts.

9. Set Sleepover Policies

Sleepovers are a high-risk event in a child's life for obvious reasons. Not only does it require you to trust the supervising adults of the home, but your child is vulnerable to the older kids who live there as well as the acting-out behaviors of any of their peers who might be struggling with sexual issues. Movie, magazine, Internet, and gaming standards vary greatly from home to home. So many children are exposed to so many different forms of abuse as well as moral temptation at these events that parents need to prayerfully and carefully choose standards and rules.

We have always held a "no sleepover" policy in our home with anyone but grandparents and aunts. I am so grateful for the grief and trauma it has prevented. Recently, I was reading Mark Gregston's blog where he strongly cautioned parents to severely limit sleepover activities. Mark, who has a weekly radio show called *Parenting Today's Teens*, works with troubled teens in his residential facility. He has heard so many stories of sleepover damages that he urges extreme caution. We have made late-night trips to retrieve our children from parties that were to become sleepovers. Sometimes it wasn't socially comfortable, but I do not regret a single trip!

10. Train for Obedience

My ability to protect my children, as we have already seen, is directly proportional to my ability to lead them and direct them. Training our children in obedience should ideally begin at birth. But anytime is still the right time to start.

Expecting them to obey your safety rules is serious business. If I tell one of my kids not to go somewhere or do something and he or she does it anyway, my discipline is swift and sure. I do not play around with disobedience. Privileges are only bestowed when trust is earned. This principle needs to begin when our children are young and extend until they are launched out of our homes.

We teach our children to expect not to understand all of our decisions. We will do our best to lead them kindly, justly, and safely. We expect their honor and obedience. If we do not receive honor and obedience, they will be demoted to the point where we can guarantee their safety. This philosophy has worked well in our home. Sitting with Mom and Dad at an activity when everyone else is free to sit with friends speaks volumes. (We could fill books with this topic here! Join us online as we work on this together.)

"But Mom, you just don't trust me!" the young teen is heard crying out. Our response: "Son, it is not about trusting you today. It is about trusting the world under the influence of darkness. And no, I do not trust those forces at all! The answer is still *no!*"

Trust the Holy Spirit to lead you. Do not over-reward or overpromote your kids beyond their proven levels of trust and maturity. Be the dad and mom and say no when the answer needs to be no!

11. Hold Your Child's Heart

Someone will hold your child's heart. According to Malachi 4, God wants the hearts of the children to be turned to the fathers lest the land will be smitten with a curse. All around us, we see evidence of the curse. Not many fathers have taken their place with their children and the mothers are scrambling to make things right. Fortunately, our God has promised to be the Father to the fatherless and a husband to the widow. (Ps. 68:5; Isa. 54:5.)

Holding our kids' hearts is special work. In the early years, it seems easy to sit them on our laps and reconnect with childlike simplicity. As they get a little older, however, and we want their world to expand, we compete against their relationships with others. That healthy balance of holding close and letting go should drive us to turn to our Daddy God for help!

The condition of your child's heart is only truly known by God. However, we can take a peek inside its chambers when our children spill words from their mouths. For Matthew 12:34 says, *"Out of the abundance of the heart the mouth speaks"* (NKJV). What are your children talking about? What names are they bringing into conversation? Whom do they dress to please? All of these answers are clues as to who is strongly influencing their hearts. Follow your gut instincts here under the leadership of the Holy Spirit and courageously ask, "Who is holding my child's heart?" You can trust Him to reveal it to you.

Obviously, a perverted man took complete hold of Kalyn's heart in the most extreme way. Yet, he did not do it overnight. He slowly chipped away at it while we were oblivious to his efforts.

Most of us, thank God, will not face that kind of full-blown attack. Most of our encounters with predatory forces will be more subtle. But how will we feel in a few years if we successfully keep our children from a molester but lose them from the body of Christ? What if instead of getting married, they cohabitate with their partners to raise our precious grandkids?

Now is the time to press into the Lord for the keys to our children's hearts! I cannot do that work for your family, and you cannot do that work for mine. But because our Father loves us so much, I am confident He is ready to teach us the way. Bringing your child back close to your heart may take sacrificial giving and supernatural patience. But what job could be more important in your lifetime?

12. Express Affection

Our children need our physical touch. Just because the world is challenged by sexual sin, do not be tricked into withholding appropriate physical affection from your child. Touch needs to be adapted to the age and personality of your child, but do not ever leave a void in his or her physical love tank. Someone else could move in to fill your void and trick your child! When we give our children the real parental affection they need, they are more equipped to recognize perverse tricks.

13. Maintain Humor

Fending off predators is hard, serious business. Living for Jesus every day takes intense focus. But that does not mean the attitude of our Christian homes should be dry, hard, boring, and stogy! Cultivate joy in your home. Make your home the place where your kids are happy to be, and you will have less other places to supervise. If your home is the fun place, friends will come to you and you will be in a position to protect while you monitor and enrich the environment. Laugh with your kids and laugh at yourself. Joy is contagious.

14. Watch Church Safety

Church safety is a huge issue deserving of a large investment of focus. Personally, I have had police officers who heard our family's story warn me that churches are among the most dangerous places for our children in America. After all, predators seek out places where children are. At first I was tempted to take offense. I love the local church and consider my fellow church members my dearest friends. This, I suppose, confirms our challenge.

As our churches communicate the love of Jesus, we welcome all people into our "church family" and allow them access to our lives and our homes. Can you see what the police officers must mean? Although there is still a threat of predators in schools and sporting centers, these venues are not as conducive to the same level of vulnerability that we have in our close-knit churches. This raises concerns for our children and youth department policies and procedures. As parents with children in our churches, we must be willing to help create and maintain strict policies, which will require *more* volunteer labor! (See links on Frontlinefamilies.org for tools available to local churches.)

I make it clear to our children that we cannot believe all people are safe just because they sit in a church pew and say they love Jesus. We assess people's safety by their attitudes, words, and behaviors. Again, remember your watch-list mentality.

15. Install a Dating/Courtship Model

How will your children find their future mates? Will your family encourage dating relationships at a young age?

When Nathan was still very young, Doug and I decided to lead our family in a courtship model. Today, two of our kids are now happily married after courting their future mates. It was a harder leadership assignment than we ever bargained for, but we would not have wanted anything less for our kids. (Our kids would love to share their romantic stories with you! Visit us at Frontlinefamilies.org for more information about courtship, dating, and preparing our kids for marriage.)

Without a vision early in childhood for the issues of dating, courtship, and marriage, how will our children recognize counterfeit ideas in our culture and how will they fend off predatory deceptions? Predators are attracted to purity. Some of the sick Internet discussions we discovered on our computer history mentioned Kalyn's innocence. We must help our kids to guard and defend their purity as something of high value and worth. We want them to be pure and innocent but not naive and vulnerable.

16. Demonstrate Marital Excitement

Marital love and sexuality is the highest model of sexual health. Our children do not just need our lectures on purity, they need to see the excitement of true love! In our home, our kids see Doug and me as romantic sweethearts. They should not be exposed to the inner bedroom of our marriage or our intimate secrets, but they should see a mom and dad excited about romantic overnight getaways and weekly date nights! They need to earnestly desire what we have and not wish they could have a secret cohabitation fling. Again, it is the issue of real versus counterfeit.

If you are a single parent or are struggling in your marriage, I strongly encourage you to intentionally seek out and expose your children to some healthy, vibrant marriages, so they can catch the vision.

17. Allow Style Expression

Standing against the cultural tide of filth is a passion of mine. To be a committed Christian means we must stand out from the crowd. But what does it mean to stand out? Does it mean we should act differently? Watch different movies? Use different language? Drink different beverages? Look different? Well, yes, yes, yes, and yes. We are, after all, citizens of a different kingdom!

How do we manage our differences while we are here in the big world? Whole denominations have spun off in an attempt to answer that question. Wrestling with these issues is inescapable for the Christian parent. The reality of the predators makes our wrestling of even higher importance.

After our battle with Kalyn, I struggled hard with these issues. Kalyn turned so deeply toward the world that my leadership in these areas was greatly challenged. But out of the pain, my view was adjusted and refined for my younger kids. I decided I would become a "cool mama."

Cool mamas venture into the fashion game with their kids rather than stand on the sideline with their whistle. Middle-aged women should not dress like teeny boppers but neither do they need to look dated and stiff! This issue goes deeper than what we adults usually recognize. Moms and Dads, we need to climb into in the ring of identity formation with our kids. They desperately need our help. The boxing around of emotions can be intense during the process, but we do not want to be seen as hanging in the opposing corner. Laughing together about the latest jean trend is a lot healthier than shouting about it in the dressing room at the mall. I've tried both.

Parents, this is an issue of the heart that I pray the Holy Spirit can get through to us. We can allow style explorations (within the boundaries of moral decency) that are not our favorites and save our no's for the bigger issues of life. When our kids are launched, let's not look back with regrets that we focused our energies on minor battles but lost the war. I can respect my daughter Hannah's developmental need to look distinctly different from her big sister Rebekah, because I am aware of the deeper issues at stake.

Let us be the first ones to compliment and encourage our children in their appearance, as well as in all other areas. Who is better equipped to instill a healthy self-image in them anyway? We must not let *anyone* take our place—for whoever takes this place will have the opportunity to feed their souls!

18. Decode the Role Models

Hugh Hefner, the king of pornography, with his latest fling with a twenty-year-old; the president and his wife; Elsie Dinsmore and her husband; Lady Gaga and her latest partner. What could these four couples possibly have in common? Each is comprised of famous people who are potential role models to our kids. How will our children properly place them in their world of experience without our help?

Perhaps you are not familiar with Elsie Dinsmore. She is a fictitious young woman from the nineteen century who is the subject of a popular series of Christian fiction for girls. When Kalyn was still angry with us for removing the predator from her life, she threw Elsie back at me, reminding me that young Elsie married a man old enough to be her father. Wow, even carefully screened Christian fiction might need some decoding for our kids!

19. Watch the Friends

"Bad company corrupts good morals" (1 Cor. 15:33 NASB). Most Christian parents are aware of this scriptural principle and work hard to steer their children toward positive influences. However, what happens if one of those positive influences turns negative?

Kalyn had always been an exceptional role model prior to her being violated; however, when the sexual-abuse side effects of rebellion, depression, and sensuality surfaced, she became a very poor influence on the kids with whom she came into contact. We called a meeting with the other parents from our church to warn them to protect their children from Kalyn. We were pulling her back from relationships but could not stop the obvious wrong messages oozing from her. How alarming that one child's encounter with a predator could traumatize and influence other children! This has serious implications for our homes and our youth ministries, and it is not easy. Sometimes we have to make strong adjustments and difficult decisions. That's part of our job as parents.

20. Monitor Cell Phones

Please remember our family's story every time you think about giving your child unsupervised use of a cell phone. Children and teenagers are quite vulnerable to the effects of fantasy. Cell phones—especially with Internet access—are a perfect doorway into a secret world. Gone are the days when young men called the house looking for a girl and had to talk to her father. Sneaking around has never been easier. And predators know this.

Texting adds another level to fantasy. You don't even have to risk someone hearing your voice, yet strong bonds can be forged. And what about the issue of sexting? Talk about a predator's playground! If your child has a cell phone, are you regularly checking the logs and texts? But even if you are, I have known many kids who routinely hid their trail from a supervising parent by erasing logs. How much technology do you want your child controlling? That is your decision as the parent. Don't fall for the "everybody is doing it" deception. Cell phones can be quite limited if a parent takes control. Covenant Eyes even has aps for mobile units. But we all know your child's friend's cell phone is but an arm's distance away and the other child's mama may not have any rules!

21. Investigate, Investigate, Investigate

If you are a twenty-first-century parent, you must become a professional private investigator. Obviously, watching for the molester is to be high on your list. However, many investigations are not as obvious but are oh, so critical. We must investigate our child's world, his culture, his friends, his personal faith formation, his interests, his passions, his fears, his temptations, his strengths, and his weaknesses. Getting inside our children's heads is equally as important as getting inside their outer worlds. This takes a great deal of ongoing effort and energy.

> Know the same people your children know, even if you have to come out of your own personal comfort zone.

Learn to ask the right probing questions without sounding like the police. (We can help you with this in our monthly POTTS video teachings.) Know the same people they know, even if you have to come out of your own personal comfort zone. Pre-approve their movies, then watch those movies with them, so you keep up with the trendy vocabulary and styles. Then you will be in a position to detect subtle changes that could indicate deception in your midst. Investigate, investigate, investigate.

22. Stay in the Word

I cannot emphasize this too much: God's Word is truth and the standard by which we can discern truth from deception. To stay sharp in our ability to know truth from error, we must *daily* sow God's Word into our spirits and our minds. I know from personal experience what happens when my Bible reading/listening habits are weak. It is amazing how quickly the deficit shows up in my mothering skills!

23. Maintain Spiritual Alertness

"*Let us not be like others, who are asleep, but let us be **alert** and self-controlled*" (1 Thess. 5:6, emphasis added). The apostle Peter wrote of the time of Jesus' return, saying, "*Prepare your minds for action; be self-controlled; set your hope fully on the grace to be given you when Jesus Christ is revealed*" (1 Pet. 1:13).

Alertness is a spiritual discipline that means to be fully aware and attentive, to have an attitude of vigilance, readiness, or caution, and to guard against danger. To be alert means to be truthful and honest in our assessments. It means to avoid overlooking, denying, wishful thinking, or naivety. It means to uncover the fire when you see the smoke. Our spirit man must be in tune with God's Spirit or we can be tricked. Learn what builds your own personal discipline of alertness, then stay on top of your game!

24. Pray

What kind of prayer is effective in protecting our kids? I would say many forms have their place and, if employed regularly, could make the difference between victory and defeat in battle. Praying scriptures, intercession, binding and loosing, and praise all have their place. The real question is...are you utilizing these tools?

25. Research Your Legal Rights

Our legal rights as parents are in question. Because of the modern "liberation" views of children and the international discussions on the rights of the child, the laws giving parents the final say in the decisions affecting their own children are shifting. As Christian parents, we must be informed.

The proposed United Nations Rights of the Child Amendment, which is embraced in theory by many countries, has been legally implemented in the Netherlands. Children are given a great deal of "freedom" and are reporting a great deal of "emotional satisfaction." As the nation lowered the age of legal consent for sexual activity to twelve years, 97 percent of their fifteen-year-old girls use contraception.[4] Are these the kinds of "freedoms" and "satisfactions" we want for our American children too? If not, we must be willing to get involved to stop the spread of these destructive decisions.

Legal and philosophical changes pose practical challenges for us as parents. The very agencies and governmental departments designed to protect our children may not, in fact, protect your parental role! Attitudes that children should be self-determining, independent decision makers have infiltrated the system as they have polluted our culture. Do you know your state's laws concerning such things as contraceptive rights or medical privacy laws for minors? I have friends who learned of these "children's rights" the hard way when the state empowered their teenage child struggling with rebellion and immorality to make independent decisions that furthered her destructive life choices.

So how do we position ourselves to honor governmental systems while not allowing our own children to become statistical casualties of a mixed-up, godless culture? That is not an easy question, but the following are a few of my thoughts.

I personally would never call a hotline or agency for help without having a good understanding of their procedures and the exact ramifications of my call. I am very grateful our criminal case did not ever move into the social service agencies for scrutiny. While I am confident Doug and I had nothing to hide from authorities, our daughter's mouth was pouring forth distorted facts that someone, in a misguided effort to "help us," could have viewed as suspicious. Remember, she thought we were the enemy—which is not unusual for a stressed teen. Could her comments of anger toward us have unleashed an investigation into our home and our parenting? Only God knows. Agencies are always made up of individuals who can apply their policies with a great deal of discretion. Researching your legal rights and pursuing legal counsel may be necessary should your family encounter a problem.

Many states have mandated reporting laws for various health professionals, counselors, teachers, clergy, or workers with children. These laws can protect our kids from predators, but they can also cause situations to spiral out of a parent's control and leave incredible room for false accusation. We must learn to operate within our rights as we cry out to our God for protection.

Do you know your laws? Are you involved in standing up to the predatory forces of darkness disguised as political actions? Check out our links on Frontlinefamilies.org for updates and ways to get involved.

26. Forgive Freely

I saved this one for last because I think it is so much a bottom line. In this battle to save our children, you may make some mistakes. Your children may disappoint you, disobey you, embarrass you, or reject you. At that moment of pain when the enemy is breathing down your back, remember the words of our Savior as He suffered on the cross: *"Father, forgive them, for they do not know what they are doing"* (Lk. 23:34).

If we will freely forgive, God is released to work on our behalf. When we grow embittered, we block God's grace and we can lose our kids.

We are living testimonies that God delivers His people! Your final chapter is not yet written. Stick with the Lord. Never, ever, *ever* give up on your kids. And let God have the final say.

As we conclude this list of twenty-six, I am reminded of a crazy idea I used to have. When Nathan and Kalyn were preschoolers, I thought my most intense years of mothering were ending since diapers were done and milk spills were fading. What a ridiculous thought. Parenting efforts do not decrease as our children grow, they just change form. To protect our children from predators will take extra work and focus!

I am excited about my future years of mothering. The opportunity to disciple the next generation thrills me. As we trust Jesus with our kids, I am confident He will preserve a new people for Himself. Will you join the ranks of frontline parents who are unmasking—and disarming—the predators?

A WORD FROM DAD

An intense personal crisis will put a man to the test. The story you have just read of my family's passage through *"the valley of the shadow of death"* stretched me almost to the point of breaking. (Ps. 23:4.) A successful family, with godly children, living the great American dream was suddenly thrust toward the rocks of destruction by a tsunami-size wave. What held the ship of my life together was an anchor for my soul. (Heb. 6:19.) That anchor held as the storms ruthlessly beat against our home for over three years.

Prior to that day in October my faith had not suffered such a test. Through the storm I found that the object of my faith was even more trustworthy than I had believed. How much better I can now relate to the words of Psalm 27:13: *"I would have despaired unless I had believed that I would see the goodness of the Lord in the land of the living"* (NASB). I know only too well what that feels like. To be in despair is to lose hope. In one of the most poignant chapters of this book (and of our life), Lisa called this "the dark night of the soul."

The best way I can explain a dark-night-of-the-soul experience is when life seems so bleak and hopeless, so void of light and so filled with despair, so purposeless and painful that it's nearly unthinkable to go on living. To reach this low point we must be confronted with a crisis that strikes at everything we are, everything we believe, and everything we love.

Lisa wrote in that "dark night" chapter that a mother's dark night is not the same as a father's dark night, and she's right.

A mother is the emotional caretaker of the family, so when the family is in severe emotional turmoil, Mom's pain is multiplied. But as the God-ordained leader of the family, the father is faced with a "buck stops here" responsibility that is enjoyable when things work but devastatingly painful when they do not.

When my daughter turned from being a loving and pleasant fifteen-year-old girl to a self-mutilating, deeply depressed, rebellious runaway, it felt like my legs had been cut out from under me. I was stunned and literally numb. How could I have allowed this to happen on my watch? What did this sudden failure say about my fathering? How could a thief have stolen my daughter from right under my nose? The pain and condemnation tried to sink me into the dark-night syndrome.

The total darkness of it all and the speed with which it happened are completely beyond my ability to express with words. "Daddy's girl" seemed to have suddenly been ripped from my hands. She was still there, in some hollow shell of a person, but the girl I had known was gone. Would I ever see her again? In a matter of thirty minutes on that incredible October day, she was morphed into a totally different human being. How could I bear it? In what seemed to be the perfect storm of pain and destruction, it was difficult to see a way out.

Visibility is so much greater on the front or the back side of a violent storm. In the midst of the tempest, it is difficult to see which way to turn. When you cannot navigate by sight, your only hope is the instrument panel. The Word of God and the leadership of the Holy Spirit miraculously guided Lisa and me through a storm that caught us completely by surprise. One morning early in the crisis—when guilt, confusion, and torment were gnawing at my inner being—I heard a quiet voice speak to me in my heart, "I will uphold your daughter by the Word of my power." I recognized those words from Hebrews 1:3 (NKJV). That moment, God laid a foundation stone on which I could stand over the next three years. That stone never gave way.

Here on the other side of the crisis I can see that what Satan meant for evil, God is using for good. My daughter is now a beacon proclaiming the light of Christ that can take this generation through incredible darkness. My wife continues to mother our children with conviction and incredible love, while helping other families to be restored. My children have experienced God's faithfulness, not just spoken of but personally witnessed in their own home. And Dad...well I have been changed to the core.

An experience that could have broken me revealed some things in my life that *needed* to be broken: pride, self-trust, independence. I still dimly remember hearing the voice of the accuser during our most desperate times of pain, darkness, and despair: "She will never come out of it. You are a failure. Your family is a farce." I am so grateful to God that through the whole process and as we proceed toward the future, we were, are, and always will be safe in His hands.

Learn from our experience. It is so much less painful to gather wisdom from the mistakes of others. I wish that we would have been better prepared. The old expression, "an ounce of prevention is worth a pound of cure," could not fit better than in the case of protecting our children from sexual predators of every kind.

TOOLS AND RESOURCES

LISA'S SCRIPTURE CONFESSION

Regularly speaking scriptures aloud is one way we get the power of God working in our situations. Hearing ourselves speak it causes faith to supernaturally rise up in our spirits, and before long we realize that we have begun to believe God's Word. (Rom. 10:17.) Because this proved to be so effective in our crisis with Kalyn, I want to share with you the confessions I spoke during that time. Actually I still speak these things every day. Through this exercise, more than any other thing I have discovered in life, I have found God to be faithful to His Word.

I encourage you to add to this list by asking the Lord to guide you to scriptures that are specific for you and your situations. Then take His Word, personalize it for yourself and your loved ones, and begin to pray it out loud. God has promised that His Word won't and can't return without producing results, but it will accomplish that for which it has been sent. (Isa. 55:11.)

For My Mind (Colossians 3:1–17)

Since, then, I have been raised with Christ, I set my heart on things above, where Christ is seated at the right hand of God. I set my mind on things above, not on earthly things. For I died and my life is now hidden with Christ in God. When Christ, who is my life, appears, then I also will appear with Him in glory.

I put to death, therefore, whatever belongs to my earthly nature: sexual immorality, impurity, lust, evil desires, and greed, which is idolatry. Because of these, the wrath of God is coming. I used to walk in these ways, in the life I once lived. But now I must rid myself of all such things as these: anger, rage, malice, slander, and filthy language from my lips. I will not lie to others, since I have taken off the old self with its practices and have put on the new self, which is being renewed in knowledge in the image of its creator. Here there is no Greek or Jew, circumcised or uncircumcised, barbarian, Scythian, slave or free, but Christ is all and is in all.

Therefore, as one of God's chosen people, holy and dearly loved, I clothe myself with compassion, kindness, humility, gentleness, and patience. I bear with others and forgive whatever grievances I have against another. I forgive as the Lord forgave me. And over all these virtues I put on love, which binds them all together in perfect unity.

I let the peace of Christ rule in my heart, since as members of one body I was called to peace. And I am thankful. I let the Word of Christ dwell in me richly as I teach and admonish others with all wisdom by singing psalms, hymns, and spiritual songs with gratitude in my heart to God. And whatever I do, whether in word or deed, I do it all in the name of the Lord Jesus, giving thanks to God the Father through Him.

I put Your covenant of increase on my mind.

For My Eyes

Like Job, I've made a covenant with my eyes. (Job 31:1.)

I ask You to open my eyes that I may see wonderful things in Your law. (Ps. 119:18.)

I lift up my eyes to the hills. Where does my help come from? My help comes from the Lord, the Maker of heaven and earth. (Ps. 121:1.)

But my eyes are fixed on You, sovereign Lord. (Ps. 141:8.)

I fix my eyes on Jesus, the author and perfecter of my faith. (Heb. 12:2.)

I fix my eyes not on what is seen but on what is unseen. (2 Cor. 4:18.)

I choose to walk by faith and not by sight. (2 Cor. 5:7.)

I will not be wise in my own eyes. I fear the Lord and shun evil. (Prov. 3:7.)

I open my eyes and look at the fields! They are ripe as to harvest. (Jn. 4:35.)

I will set before my eyes no worthless thing. I hate the work of those who fall away. (Ps. 101:3.)

My Ears

I am quick to listen, slow to speak, and slow to become angry. (James 1:19.)

I am a wise woman for I listen to advice. (Prov. 12:15.)

I am Jesus' sheep, and I listen to His voice; the voice of a stranger I simply do not listen to. (Jn. 10:5, 27.)

Speak, Lord, for I, Your servant, am listening. (1 Sam. 3:9.)

My Mouth

You've put a new song in my mouth, a hymn of praise to my God. (Ps. 40:3.)

His praise will always be on my lips. (Ps. 34:1.)

May my lips overflow with praise. (Ps. 119:171.)

I will put a muzzle on my mouth, and I will keep my tongue from sin. (Ps. 39:1.)

I will not let this Book of the Law depart from my mouth. (Josh. 1:8.)

I keep my lips from speaking lies. (Ps. 34:13.)

I keep a tight rein on my tongue. (James 1:26.)

No man can tame the tongue, but the Lord is my help. (James 3:8; Heb. 4:16.)

I have wisdom, she is my sister; and the tongue of the wise brings healing. (Prov. 7:4; 12:18.)

I only speak that which is good to edify. (Eph. 4:29.)

I dwell in the shelter of the Most High and I will rest in the shadow of the Almighty.

I will say of the Lord, "He is my refuge and my fortress, my God, in whom I trust."

Surely He will save me from the fowler's snare and from the deadly pestilence.

He will cover me with His feathers, and under His wings I will find refuge.

His faithfulness will be my shield and rampart.

I will not fear the terror of night, nor the arrow that flies by day, nor the pestilence that stalks in the darkness, nor the plague that destroys at midday.

A thousand may fall at my side, ten thousand at my right hand, but it will not come near me.

I will only observe with my eyes and see the punishment of the wicked.

If I make the Most High my dwelling—even the Lord, who is my refuge, then no harm will befall me, no disaster will come near my tent.

For He will command His angels concerning me to guard me in all my ways.

They will lift me up in their hands, so that I will not strike my foot against a stone.

I will tread upon the lion and the cobra; I will trample the great lion and the serpent.

Because I love the Lord, He says He will rescue me.

He will protect me, for I acknowledge His name.

I will call upon Him, and He will answer me;

He will be with me in trouble; He will deliver me and honor me.

With long life He will satisfy me and show me His salvation. (Psalm 91.)

My words are aptly spoken like apples of gold in settings of silver. (Prov. 25:11.)

My "No'se"

Whatever I bind on earth will be bound in heaven. (Matt. 16:19.) I say no to:

(List whatever the Lord puts on your heart for you and your family's situation. The following are some ideas.)

- Sin
- Worry
- Fear
- Terror
- Devil
- Rebellion
- Sickness and Disease
- Accidents
- Poverty
- Mental Torment
- Oppression
- Depression
- Unproductivity
- Confusion
- Idolatry
- Pride
- Self-will
- Lust
- Bondage
- Wrong Dating Relationships
- Wrong Friendships
- Gluttony
- Eating Disorders
- Food Addictions
- Poor Self-image
- Roots of Rejection
- Sibling Rivalry
- Slothfulness
- Laziness
- Disorderliness
- Intimidation
- Man-pleasing
- Contemplation
- Condemnation
- Strife
- Doubt
- Unbelief
- Immodest Dress
- Selfishness
- Overspending
- Marital Conflict
- Nagging

I say yes to the blessings over my family. Deuteronomy 28 says:

If we fully obey the Lord our God and carefully follow all His commands we are given today, the Lord our God will set us high above all the nations on earth. All these blessings will come upon us and accompany us if we obey the Lord our God:

We will be blessed in the city and blessed in the country.

The fruit of our womb will be blessed, and the crops of our land and the young of our livestock—the calves of our herds and the lambs of our flocks.

Our basket and our kneading trough will be blessed.

We will be blessed when we come in and blessed when we go out.

The Lord will grant that the enemies who rise up against us will be defeated before us. They will come at us from one direction but flee from us in seven.

The Lord will send a blessing on our barns and on everything we put our hands to. The Lord our God will bless us in the land He is giving us.

The Lord will establish us as His holy people, as He promised us on oath, if we keep the commands of the Lord our God and walk in His ways. Then all the peoples on earth will see that we are called by the name of the Lord, and they will fear us. The Lord will grant us abundant prosperity—in the fruit of our womb, the young of our livestock, and the crops of our ground—in the land He swore to our forefathers to give us.

The Lord will open the heavens, the storehouse of His bounty, to send rain on our land in season and to bless all the work of our hands. We will lend to many nations but will borrow from none. The Lord will make us the head, not the tail. If we pay attention to the commands of the Lord our God that He gives us this day and carefully follow them, we will always be at the top, never at the bottom. We do not turn aside from any of the commands He gives us today, to the right or the left, following other gods and serving them.

I abide in the vine! (Jn. 15:4.)

My Heart

I have no fear of bad news, my heart is steadfast. (Ps. 112:7.)

I watch over my heart with all diligence for from it flow the springs of life. (Prov. 4:23.)

I love the Lord my God with all my heart, soul, and mind. (Matt. 22:37.)

I fix these words of Yours in my heart. (Deut. 11:18.)

I do not harden my heart. (Heb. 3:8.)

Search me, O God, and know my heart. (Ps. 139:23.)

Create in me a pure heart, O God, and renew a right spirit within me. (Ps. 51:10.)

A broken and contrite heart You will not despise. (Ps. 51:17.)

Give me, Lord, an undivided heart. (Ps. 86:11.)

May the meditation of my heart be pleasing to You. (Ps. 19:14.)

I thank You, Lord, that You are greater than my heart. (1 Jn. 3:20.)

I pour out my heart to You. (Ps. 62:8.)

I do not let my heart be troubled. (Jn. 14:1.)

I have set my heart on pilgrimage. (Ps. 84:5.)

A cheerful heart is good medicine—I stir up the joy. (Prov. 17:22.)

Thank You that You heal my heart when it is broken and bind up my wounds. (Ps. 147:3.)

My Hands

Who may ascend your holy hill, he who has clean hands and a pure heart. (Ps. 24:3–4.)

I lift up holy hands in prayer. (1 Tim. 2:8.)

My times are in Your hands, O God. (Ps. 31:15.)

I do not fear for You uphold me by Your righteous right hand. (Isa. 41:10.)

I have laid my hands to the plow, I do not look back. (Lk. 9:62.)

Ephesians 6:13–18

Therefore I put on the full armor of God, so that when the day of evil comes, I may be able to stand my ground, and after I have done everything, to stand. I stand firm then, with the belt of truth buckled around my waist, with the breastplate of righteousness in place, and with my feet fitted with the readiness that comes from the gospel of peace. In addition to all this, I take up the shield of faith, with which I can extinguish all the flaming arrows of the evil one. I take the helmet of salvation and the sword of the Spirit, which is the Word of God. And I pray in the Spirit on all occasions with all kinds of prayers and requests. With this in mind, I am alert and always keep on praying for all the saints.

My Feet

You've set my feet upon a rock. (Ps. 40:2.)

Your Word is a lamp to my feet. (Ps. 119:105.)

How beautiful are my feet for I am bringing good news. (Rom. 10:15.)

I am going into all the world, preaching the good news, making disciples of all nations, baptizing them in the name of the Father, Son, and Holy Spirit. (Matt. 28:19.)

Like Joshua, every place the soles of my feet tread belongs to me. (Josh. 1:3.)

I'm taking dominion and authority to trample on snakes and scorpions and over all the power of the enemy. (Lk. 10:19.)

I do not let the sun go down on my anger, and I do not give the devil a foothold. (Eph. 4:26–27.)

My feet are shod with the preparation of the gospel of peace. (Eph. 6:15.)

I'm taking the path of righteousness, following the blood of the martyrs. (Prov. 2:20; Rev. 16:6).

I overcome by the blood of the lamb, the word of my testimony, and I love not my own life even unto death. (Rev. 12:11.)

AMEN.

Tool 2

LISA'S JOURNAL—DECEMBER 2002

This is the actual entry from my journal that day when we were so desperate for help in leading Kalyn. I have included it here in its entirety to encourage you to seek the Lord for your battle plans. Notice the precision of God's instructions and the accuracy of His assessments! I am confident He will help your family also.

"Lord, what are we to do?" I asked.

"Cut it off! Let Me pursue," He said.

My response to Him: "I can see it, Lord. You did not cause this. It's an attack from the enemy, but You will use this for good in our lives. I must give her over to this season of her life to kill off the root of rebellion—to God, His Word, and earthly authorities."

This trial is also a season of pruning for Doug and for me. I've tried complaining, rebelling, compromising, and running away. This pruning is about me placing upon the altar (or allowing to be killed off in me):

* *A "perfect" family image*

* *My kids being perfect, mature, high achievers for my glory*

* *My self-sufficiency*

* *My motherhood ambitions as a source of significance*

* *My ministry as a source of my significance*

* *My right to know, reason, and control timing and seasons of life*

* *My family's and friends' approval, understanding, or help*

* *My allowing "individuating" without fear of change (i.e. development of each child's individual identity)*

* *My trusting in God to send His fire to my children*

* *My personal needs for love, acceptance, or approval from Kalyn—or my other children.*

Instruction from the Lord: "We must have No Compromise—No Fear—No Condemnation."

What we could not accomplish in her—God will accomplish. We must not "go down to Egypt" for help. We must lay it out for her (renounce worldly counsel) and help her to understand the teen year challenges she is in and that we understand and recognize her pain but hold fast to only one relief valve—God's Word and His ways. Just as what Kalyn was looking for in that man could only be found in Jesus, what I'm looking for in "calling Doug" can only be found in Jesus!

Growing edge to learn from the Lord:

* In issues of style, preference, give her room

vs.

* In issues of modesty and vision and godly direction, give her no room

She is in an identity crisis. An identity crisis is always a spiritual crisis.

Then I sensed God speaking these words to me: "See her as delivered. See her as set free. Treat her as such. Pray the prayer of faith. Ignore symptoms. Walk in wisdom concerning the day to day. Watch My Word performed in your midst. The victory is yours, the battle is Mine. Quit battling and walk it out. Go to Higher places.

"Declare and decree My Word. It is your intercession. Receive the flow of love. Fight the battle, as you have already been prepared. Cancel the negative words over Kalyn. She is an obedient child. Celebrate each moment of victory. Encourage her whole heart. This is a cancer in her soul."

This is the picture I saw:

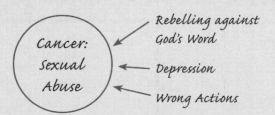

"Cut off the metastases of the cancer—false counsels, false relationships, false teachings."

I asked the Lord: "Why did she develop the cancer?" He answered me: "She had a weak immune system: Her love tank is low from Mom and Dad. She feels a root of rejection from Mom. She feels low self-esteem. This is a spiritual crisis with identity confusion and rebellion not dealt with—also envy and jealousy.

"Many of these weaknesses are developmental: i.e. adolescent brain immaturities, growing up issues, faith development issues, and individuation. But some are wounds like rejection from the abuse. Pray for healing over these wounds. Some are sin such as rebellion and envy. Strengthen her immune system now: her spirit identity, her love from God and parents. Take control over your child. Be her outer control until her inner controls have healed. Protect her from herself, from attracting others who are dangerous. Protect her emotionally.

"Prepare for Me to do a surgical removal of the cancer [the abuse wound]—it needs precision accuracy. It needs skill. Learn so you can intercede with her in her present sense of reality. This was abuse of a child, so it is very complicating to her current and future development. Let her build a new life."

NOTES

Introduction

1. Eliot J. Briere, "Prevalance and Psychological Sequelae of Self-Reported Childhood Physical and Sexual Abuse in the General Population," *Child Abuse and Neglect* 27 (2003), 1205–1222, www.johnbriere.com/CAN%20csa%20cpa.pdf. (Accessed January 27, 2012.)

2. N. K. Gartrell, H. M. W. Bos, N. G. Goldberg, *Archive Sexual Behavior*, "New Trends in Same-Sex Sexual Contact for American Adolescents?" (Springer Science+Business Media, LLC, 2011), http://www.nllfs.org/images/uploads/pdf/nllfs-letter-editor-december-2011.pdf. (Accessed December 27, 2011.)

3. Sharon Jayson, "Teens Define Sex In New Ways," *USA Today-Health and Behavior* (October 19, 2005), http://www.usatoday.com/news/health/2005-10-18-teens-sex_x.htm. (Accessed January 26, 2012.)

4. Sharon Jayon, Barna Research Group, "A New Generation of Adults Bends Moral and Sexual Rules to Their Liking" (Ventura, CA: Barna Group, October 31, 2006), http://www.barna.org/barna-update/article/13-culture/144-a-new-generation-of-adults-bends-moral-and-sexual-rules-to-their-liking?q=pornography. (Accessed December 27, 2011.)

Chapter 3

1. John Gill, *The New John Gill Exposition on the Entire Bible*, "Commentary on James 1:17," http://www.studylight.org/com/geb/view.cgi?book=jas&chapter=001&verse=017,s.v."with. (Accessed February 2012.)

2. See Psalm 12:7; Proverbs 18:10; and 1 John 5:18.

3. See Matthew 28:20 and Luke 21:27.

4. TeenHelp.Com, "Teen Depression Statistics," http://www.teenhelp.com/teen-depression/depression-statistics.html. (Accessed May 2011.)

5. Centers for Disease Control and Prevention, "Injury Prevention & Control: Data & Statistics Web-based Injury Statistics Query and Reporting System," (Atlanta, GA: 2007), http://www.cdc.gov/injury/wisqars/index.html. (Accessed January 24, 2012.)

6. A. Derouin and T. Bravender, "Living on the Edge: Self-Mutilation in Adolescents," *MCN: The American Journal of Maternal/Child Nursing Special Issue on Adolescents* 29, vol. 1 (2004), 12–18.

7. "Youth Risk Behavior Surveillance—United States, 2009," *Morbidity Mortality Weekly Report* (2010) 59 (SS-5):1–142, http://www.cdc.gov/mmwr/pdf/ss/ss5905.pdf, quoted in CDC, http://www.cdc.gov/HealthyYouth/sexualbehaviors/. (Accessed May 2011.)

8. William Mosher, Anjani Chandra, and Jo Jones, "Sexual Behavior and Selected Health Measures: Men and Women 15–44 Years of Age, United States, 2002," *Advance Data from Vital and Health Statistics* 362 (September 15, 2005), http://www.cdc.gov/nchs/data/ad/ad362.pdf. (Accessed January 24, 2012.)

9. Guttmacher Institute, "U.S. Teenage Pregnancies, Births and Abortions: National and State Trends and Trends by Race and Ethnicity," (January, 2010): 3, http://www.guttmacher.org/pubs/ustrends.pdf. (Accessed January 24, 2012.)

10. Josh McDowell and David Bellis. *The Last Christian Generation,* (Holiday, FL: Green Key Books, 2006), 17.

11. Ron Luce, *ReCreate: Building a Culture in Your Home Stronger than the Culture Deceiving Your Kids* (Ventura, CA: Regal, 2008), 12.

12. Based on information from *Strong's Hebrew Lexicon*, s.v. "mother," Genesis 2:24, http://www.eliyah.com/cgi-bin/strongs.cgi?file=hebrewlexicon&isindex=517.

13. Based on information from Anabel Gillham, *The Confident Woman: Knowing Who You Are in Christ* (Eugene, OR: Harvest House, 2003).

Chapter 4

1. The Literature Network, "Sun Tzu" biography, http://www. online-literature.com/suntzu/. (Accessed January 4, 2012.)

2. The Dictionary.com, "deceive," http://dictionary.reference. com/browse/deceive. (Accessed January 4, 2012).

3. Josh McDowell and David H. Bellis, *The Last Christian Generation* (Holiday, FL: Green Key Books, 2006), 13.

4. Thom Rainer, *The Bridger Generation* (Nashville: B & H Publishing Group, 2006), 169.

5. Thom S. Rainer and Jess W. Rainer, *The Millennials: Connecting to America's Largest Generation* (Nashville: Broadman and Holman, 2011) 244.

6.Guttmacher Institute, "An Overview of Abortion in the United States," http://www.guttmacher.org/media/presskits/2005/06/28/ abortionoverview.html. (Accessed December, 2009).

7. Thayer and Smith, "Greek Lexicon entry for Skotos," s.v. "darkness," Acts 26:18, http://www.biblestudytools.net/Lexicons/ Greek/grk.cgi?number=4655&version=kjv.

Chapter 5

1. The Barna Group, "A New Generation of Adults Bends Moral and Sexual Rules to Their Liking." (See Note 4, Introduction.)

2. Josh McDowell and Bob Hostetler, *Beyond Belief to Convictions* (Wheaton, IL: Tyndale House, 2002), 12.

3. Ibid., 12–13.

4. The Barna Group, "Most American Christians Do Not Believe that Satan or the Holy Spirit Exist" (April, 2009), paragraph 5, http://www.barna.org/barna-update/article/12-faithspirituality/260-most-american-christians-do-not-believe-that-satan-or-the-holy-spirit-exist.

5. Based on information from *Strong's Exhaustive Concordance of the Bible*, http://www.eliyah.com/cgi-bin/strongs.cgi?file=greekle xicon&isindex=1849.

Also Thayer and Smith, *The KJV New Testament Greek Lexicon*, "Greek Lexicon entry for Exousia," http://www.biblestudytools.net/ Lexicons/Greek/grk.cgi?number=1849&version=kjv.

6. Thayer and Smith, "Greek Lexicon entry for Exousia," http://www.biblestudytools.net/Lexicons/Greek/grk. cgi?number=1849&version=kjv.

7. *Beyond Belief to Convictions*, 11–12.

8. Barna Research Group, "Barna Survey Examines Changes in Worldview Among Christians over the Past 13 Years" (March 6, 2009), http://barna.org/barna-update/article/21-transformation/252-barna-survey-examines-changes-in-worldview-among-christians-over-the-past-13-years.

9. Ron Luce, *ReCreate: Building a Culture in Your Home Stronger than the Culture Deceiving Your Kids* (Ventura, CA: Regal, 2008), 27.

Chapter 6

1. Fictious husband and wife in the TV sitcom, *Leave It to Beaver*.

Chapter 7

1. For more information on what should be said during a disclosure of abuse, see Cynthia Kubetin and James Mallory, *Beyond the Darkness—Healing for Victims of Sexual Abuse* (Dallas: Rapha Publishing/Word, Inc., 1992), 216, 219.

2. "My Hope Is Built," words by Edward Mote, music by William B. Bradley; first published in 1836.

3. *Webster's New Collegiate Dictionary* (Springfield, Massachusetts: G & C Merriam Co., 1974), s.v. "condemnation."

4. Ibid, s.v. "conviction."

5. Gary Smalley, *The DNA of Relationships* (Wheaton, IL: Tyndale House, 2004), 83.

Chapter 8

1. Amy Carmichael, http://www.christianadoption.com/ renewingthemind/fame.htm, quoted from Ellen Sanna, *God's Hall of Fame* (Urichsville,OH: Barbour Publishing, 1999).

2 .Bruce Wilkerson, *Secrets of the Vine: Breaking Through to Abundance* (Sisters, OR: Multnomah Books, 2006).

3. Norman Grubb, *Rees Howells: Intercessor* (Fort Washington, PA: CLC Ministries, 1997).

4. Dan B. Allender, *The Wounded Heart: Hope for Adult Victims of Childhood Sexual Abuse* (Colorado Springs: Navpress, 2008), 46–49.

5. Joyce Meyer is a well-known Christian author, Bible teacher, and speaker. Her *Emotional Healing Kit* is available through her ministry or online at http://www.joycemeyer.org/eStore/default.htm.

Chapter 9

1. Thayer and Smith, "Greek Lexicon entry for Agape," s.v. "love," 1 Corinthians 3:4, http://www.biblestudytools.net/Lexicons/ Greek/grk.cgi?number=26&version=kjv.

2. Dr. S. M. Davis, *How to Win the Heart of a Rebel* (Oak Brook, IL: IBLP, CD format), available from http://store.iblp.org/products/ CWHR/.

3. Michael J. Bradley, *Yes, Your Teen Is Crazy* (Gig Harbor, Washington: Harbor Press, 2006).

4. Joyce Meyer, *The Everyday Life Bible—Amplified Version* (New York: FaithWords, 2006), 1585.

Chapter 11

1. Dan B. Allender, *The Wounded Heart: Hope for Adult Victims of Childhood Sexual Abuse* (Colorado Springs: Navpress, 2008), 48.

2. Ibid., 51.

3. The Dictionary.com, "ab ," http://dictionary.reference.com/ browse/deceive. (Accessed January 4, 2012).

3. Douglas Harper, Historian, Dictionary.com *Online Etymology Dictionary,* "ab," http://dictionary.reference.com/browse/ab. (Accessed: January 04, 2012.)

4. Eliot J. Briere, "Prevalance and Psychological Sequelae of Self-Reported Childhood Physical and Sexual Abuse in the General Population," *Child Abuse and Neglect* 27 (2003) 1205–1222, www. johnbriere.com/CAN%20csa%20cpa.pdf.

5. Kathryn Brohl and Joyce Case Potter, *When Your Child Has Been Molested: A Parent's Guide to Healing and Recovery* (San Francisco, CA: Josssey-Bass, 2004), 4–6.

6. U.S. Department of Health and Human Services, "Statutory Rape: A Guide to State Laws and Reporting Requirements Summary of Current State Laws," http://aspe.hhs.gov/hsp/08/SR/ StateLaws/summary.shtml#top. (Accessed January 24, 2012.)

7. Jade Christine Angelica, *We Are Not Alone: A Guidebook for Helping Professionals and Parents Supporting Adolescent Victims of Sexual Abuse* (New York: Haworth Press, 2002), 5.

8. *When Your Child Has Been Molested: A Parent's Guide to Healing and Recovery,* 4–6.

9. *The Wounded Heart: Hope for Adult Victims of Childhood Sexual Abuse,* 157-169.

10. Carla van Dam, *Identifying Child Molesters: Preventing Child Sexual Abuse by Recognizing the Patterns of the Offenders* (New York: Haworth Press, 2002), 137-180.

11. Ibid.

12. Kenneth V. Lanning, *Child Molesters: A Behavioral Analysis,* National Center for Missing and Exploited Children, Office of Juvenile Justice and Delinquency Prevention: U.S. Department of Justice—Office of Justice Programs and Federal Bureau of Investigation (September, 2001), fourth edition, 15–24.

13. Ibid.

14. Ibid., 14–15.

15. H. N. Snyder (2000). *Sexual Assault of Young Children as Reported to Law Enforcement: Victim, Incident, and Offender Characteristics,* NCJ 182990 Washington, DC, U.S. Department of Justice Programs, Bureau of Justice statistics, http://bjs.ojp.usdoj. gov/content/pub/pdf/saycrle.pdf, 8. (Accessed January 4, 2012.)

16. *When Your Child Has Been Molested: A Parent's Guide to Healing and Recovery,* 4–6.

17. *Child Molesters: A Behavioral Analysis,* 19–30.

18. *Sexual Assault of Young Children as Reported to Law Enforcement: Victim, Incident, and Offender Characteristics,* 9–10.

19. A. J. Sedlak, J. Mettenburg, M. Basena, I. Petta, K. McPherson, A. Greene, and S. Li, *Fourth National Incidence Study of Child Abuse and Neglect* (NIS-4): Report to Congress, Executive Summary (Washington, D.C.: U. S. Department of Health & Human Services, Administration for Children and Families, 2010).

20. Shannon M. Catalino, "Criminal Victimization, 2005," US Department of Justice, Bureau of Statistics, 2006, 4–11, http://bjs. gov/content/pub/pdf/cv05.pdf. (Accessed January 26, 2012.)

21. D.W. Smith, E. J. Letourneau, B. E. Saunders, D. G. Kilpatrick, H. S. Resnick, and C.L. Best, "Delay in Disclosure of Childhood Rape: Results from a National Survey," *Child Abuse & Neglect,* 24 (2000), 273–287.

22. J. J. Broman-Fulks, K. J. Ruggiero, R. F. Hanson, D. W. Smith, H. S. Resnick, D. G. Kilpatrick, and B. E. Saunders, "Sexual Assault Disclosure in Relation to Adolescent Mental Health: Results from the National Survey of Adolescents," *Journal of Clinical Child and Adolescent Psychology,* 36 (2007), 260–266.

23. "Delay in Disclosure of Childhood Rape: Results from a National Survey," 273–287.

24. Dictionary.com, "detect," http://dictionary.reference.com/browse/detect. (Accessed January 04, 2012.)

25. Cynthia Kubetin and James Mallory, *Beyond the Darkness* (Houston/Dallas, Texas: Rapha Publishing/Word Publishing, 1992), 4–5.

26. Darkness to Light, "How Many Child Sexual Abuse Perpetrators Go To Jail?" http://www.d2l.org/site/c.4dICIJOkGcISE/b.6250805/k.E0A3/How_Many_Child_Sexual_Abuse_Perpetrators_Go_To_Jail.htm. (Accessed January 4, 2011.)

Chapter 12

1. H. N. Snyder (2000). *Sexual Assault of Young Children as Reported to Law Enforcement: Victim, Incident, and Offender Characteristics,* NCJ 182990 Washington, DC, U.S. Department of Justice Programs, Bureau of Justice statistics, http://bjs.ojp.usdoj.gov/content/pub/pdf/saycrle.pdf, 6. (Accessed January 4, 2012.)

2. Gary Chapman and Ross Campbell, *The Five Love Languages of Children* (Chicago: Northfield, 1997).

3. Mark Gregston, *Parenting Today's Teens,* "Teens and Sleepovers," Program Archives (June 21, 2012), http://www.heartlightministries.org/blogs/pttradio/2010/06/22/teens-sleepovers-6212010/. (Accessed January 4, 2012.)

4. Peter Kamakawiwoole, ParentalRights.org, *The Netherlands: A Child-Centered Society* (November 25, 2008), http://www.parentalrights.org/index.asp?Type=B_BASIC&SEC={E9FBC365-21EA-45E3-8218-DC49B88DA8AE}&DE=. (Accessed January 4, 2012.)

ABOUT THE AUTHORS

Lisa Cherry and her daughter Kalyn Cherry Waller have navigated the storm of extreme family crises and spiritual warfare and emerged as a victorious voice for others. Their ministry has placed them on the front lines speaking to tens of thousands of parents and teens each year. Their message acts as a beacon of light and hope to aid parents and teens with practical communication tools to avoid crises such as child predators.

Championing the cause of better family communication and spiritual growth, Lisa and her husband, Doug, are founders of Frontline Family Ministries, which is dedicated to providing communication tools and practical resources for growing spiritual and healthy families.

Lisa and Doug are the proud parents of ten children and four grandchildren.

Kalyn and her husband, Adam, are Mom and Dad to Kyla Grace Waller.

As passionate servants of Christ, the Cherry family founded Victory Dream Center and live in Carbondale, Illinois.

CONTACT US!

We would love to hear from you! Contact Lisa or Kalyn at:

Frontline Family Ministries
P.O. Box 460
Carbondale, IL 62903

Lisa@frontlinefamilies.org
Kalyn@frontlinefamilies.org
800 213 9899 or **618 525 2025**

FRONTLINEFAMILIES.ORG

Growing spiritual and healthy families

- ❖ *Unmask the Predators* DVD curriculum for home or small group use
- ❖ Daily online tips for parents
- ❖ Resources for parents and teens
- ❖ Timely topics for families
- ❖ DVDs, books, CDs
- ❖ Lisa's blog for moms
- ❖ Doug's blog for dads
- ❖ Prayer support
- ❖ Parent coaching

To schedule Lisa, Kalyn, or Doug to speak for your church, parent organization, women's conference, or youth event, call **800.213.9899** or **618.525.2025** or e-mail us at **Lisa@ Frontlinefamilies.org** or **Kalyn@Frontlinefamilies.org**.

POTTS
PARENTS OF TEENS AND TWEENS

Join the ranks of Christian parents
standing shoulder to shoulder.

Growing Spiritual and Healthy Families

We are a national organization with local groups in churches and communities supporting, strengthening, and equipping parents of the next generation of Christ followers.

- ✧ Resources and training materials
- ✧ Monthly video seminars for families and groups
- ✧ Online and personal representatives for equipping local groups
- ✧ Prayer support and encouragement for families
- ✧ Daily tips for parents called *Bites*
- ✧ Speakers for local churches, groups, conferences, or events.
- ✧ Regional Parenting Conferences in conjunction with Acquire the Fire in cities all across America. Check for a conference near you **www.acquirethefire.com**.

To join us as a family, start a local group, or schedule a speaker for your event, go to **POTTSgroup.com** or follow the link on **Frontlinefamilies.org**. or call **800.213.9899** or **618.525.2025**.